Freedom
from *Depression*

**No Matter What
Your *Disability* May Be**

Cynthia Lee De Boer

OpenHeart Press

We Can Create Heaven on Earth, We Can Create Hell on Earth— It's all up to us!
By Cynthia L. De Boer

ENDORSEMENTS

"That Cynthia L. De Boer is a talented author, there is no doubt. In this most recent book she pays careful attention to provide step-by-step guidelines for challenging the engulfing force of depression. In outlining her life challenges, Cynthia develops a road map for everyone confronting issues surrounding a personal disability. This inspiring, well-written book is a focused life-style path for positive approaches in dealing with the emotional aspects of a disability. Medical professionals would be well advised to use this format as a teaching tool and personal guidebook when assisting clients dealing with the broad aspects of a disability."

Joyce K. Walters, R.N., M.S.
www.LinesofListeningBlog.Wordpress.com

"I happened to read Cynthia's book when I was feeling overworked and discouraged with my personal business endeavors, and it provided a much-appreciated uplift and inspiration. The combination of personal stories, quotes, tips, and writing exercises provided me with several practical options that directly reduced the stress and worry I was experiencing, allowing me to re-center myself in a more positive frame of thinking. Thank you."

Jenny Ballif
https://jennyballif.com

••••••••••••••••••••••••••••••••••

"Cynthia De Boer's story is nothing short of inspirational. Coping with physical disability can be difficult for oneself as well as one's family and friends. This book will surely take you through an emotional journey to come out stronger."

Janet Chao, BCO, CCA
www.prostheticslab.com

••••••••••••••••••••••••••••••••••

"When I read Cynthia's first book regarding her life with a prosthetic eye I actually found myself cheering her on when she overcame one obstacle after another, it was that inspirational. Every roadblock that stood in front was vanquished to keep moving forward with a strong positive attitude. Positive thinking is one of the gifts given to us but it is also one of the gifts we probably do not use enough. After reading the trials and tribulations Cynthia has endured, I consider her second book the weaponry she used to conquer the challenges and overcome defeat. Depression is not uncommon; I believe everyone on earth has been depressed at one time or another in his or her life. Cynthia has put together a splendid book to battle depression, to show how positive thinking can change and improve your world and the others in it. The book, or should I say this manual for better living, gives us the weapons, (or if you like the word 'tools' better), to improve our lives and overcome depression. Whether you consider yourself a positive thinker or not, her new book should be required reading not only for yourself but for the whole family as well. I just wish I had this book earlier in life. Keep storming the castle, Cyndi; with your help the positive will always overcome the negative."

Gary Buyachek

*Historical Document/
Ephemera Collector & Seller*

"Freedom from Depression is very inspiring. Cynthia De Boer demonstrates how she was able to 'Turn Pain into Purpose.' A loss is never really a loss if you learned a lesson. The lesson could be a blessing to someone else."

Shameka 'Meme' Green
Author of Beauty from Ashes and Owner of Emma's House Inc.
A Self-empowerment Program for Women

"Cynthia De Boer's *Freedom from Depression: No Matter What Your Disability May Be* is a lovingly conceived compendium of LIFE and how to navigate it. Her target audience is those with any type of disability that would cause their daily existence to be stressful, thus leading to possible depression. However, this is not a depressing book!! It is filled with tried and true activities to combat the struggles facing us all. Cynthia has parlayed her considerable mental and physical challenges into an uplifting how-to book that instructs, encourages and entertains. Thank you, Cynthia, for bravely allowing us into your daily triumph to face and defeat negativity and self-doubt. I would recommend your book to all who believe life should be cherished—no matter the circumstances."

Jane Dow

Friend and mentor

"After 30 years of friendship Cynthia never ceases to amaze me with her talents and insights. This is a great inspirational book and I believe it can be very helpful to many people, great ideas and insights in how to make your life easier and brighter. She is an amazing author and an even more amazing person. Enjoy the read because I am sure you will read it more than once."

Rickey Stewart

"Cynthia De Boer has been a victor over her physical disabilities. We know that from reading her previous book, *Me, Myself and Eye*. Now Cynthia shares methods she uses to overcome depression before it can take control. The workbook style of Cynthia's book makes it more helpful than any I have seen. We all know folks who struggle with depression. This is a practical and welcome tool to give help to them. I feel all who read and use it will be blessed with a better mental outlook."

Sharon Peterson,
Former Flight Attendant
Writer and Bible Studies Teacher

"Fun and enjoyable to read, this book is filled with tons of great advice that is simple to implement for any lifestyle."

James F. Rea III
Las Vegas Business Owner and Independent Filmmaker

"Cynthia's book is very impressive. She is able to pinpoint our human frailties, and emotions, which are common among all of us. She writes in a manner that is very easy for us to equate with. From her point of view with all the challenges she's faced in her life. She has a very unique perspective that we can connect with. This book is very easy to read, and if we let it can make very definite changes in our life's. This book touched my soul. I was very moved. I highly recommend this book."

Linda Korfman

Volunteer, Freedom Hooves Therapeutic Riding Center Wichita, Kansas, Facebook

"'We are our brothers' (and I'll say sisters' too!) keepers.' This I have come to believe in, now more devoutly than ever in my years in life. I find that Cynthia's honest, bravely revealing, heartfelt writing of her personal travails and shared insights has provided me with some deeper sense of our roles in life to consider as brothers' and sisters' keepers — but not only that! This book positively raises one's cognitive level of their own situation, but also educates us to consider, more than ever, other's struggles in life and how we can positively counter them. There is absolutely a definite interplay of our level of self-cognizance, how we affect others, and are affected by others' struggles in life. In today's stressful times, we can see much benefit to taking deeper breaths and more time to consider others' situations before reacting in our usual self-gratifying ways that lead to only regrets. Next time you see someone pull out too far from the driveway into your lane in traffic, don't lay into your horn forever after you already made leeway for the person to enter! You see, your situation that makes you react negatively may not be so different to the other person's situation that caused them to pull out so (apparently not so dangerously far) into your traffic lane."

Allan Charak

Freedom from Depression

Also by

Cynthia L. De Boer

ME, MYSELF AND EYE

THE REALITIES OF LIVING

WITH A PROSTHETIC EYE

Freedom from Depression, No Matter What Your Disability May Be

Cynthia Lee De Boer

© 2018 by Cynthia Lee De Boer

All rights reserved.

No part of this book may be reproduced in any form or by any electronic or mechanical means including information storage and retrieval systems, without permission in writing from the author. The only exception is by a reviewer, who may quote short excerpts in a review.

ISBN-13: 978-1-7321384-0-7

Printed in USA

CONTENTS

Dedication	29
Acknowledgments	31
Introduction	35
SECTION ONE My Journey and the Need to Live in the Positive	41
SECTION TWO Teachable Moments	65
SECTION THREE Comforting Ideas	135
SECTION FOUR Your Groundwork	157
SECTION FIVE Information and FAQs — To Build Understanding	203
Dear Reader	215
Index	217
About the Author	223

DEDICATION

To my family with love
and gratitude
Cynthia L. De Boer

ACKNOWLEDGMENTS

As I have stated many times, we are not on this earthly journey alone. Amazing people have blessed my life, from my parents to complete strangers. Every person offered me a new role to fulfill and fresh ways to experience and appreciate life.

Regarding my roles as an author and inspirational speaker, I feel the following quote from Mark Twain sums it up: "The two most important days in your life are the day you were born … and the day you find out why." My career is a big part of my why and speaking with a complete stranger revealed it. By sharing my knowledge with this stranger, she viewed her new monocular world in a less frightening and more positive light. In return, this single conversation changed the course of my life. My path to help others is paved with the stories of my life. No, I am not famous, rich or someone holding numerous degrees, instead I gained my knowledge and insight through the school of life, from facing challenges, from making mistakes and from rising after every failure to try again. I am an ordinary person, proof to all the other ordinary people that we are all truly extraordinary human beings!

My heartfelt gratitude goes to the stranger who touched my life, my friends and fellow authors, the dedicated and talented staff at Imagine Communications including Brian Rouff, Managing Partner; Cynthia Carbajal, cover design; Julie Varley, layout design; author's photo, Rick Trelease; and my editor, Jami Carpenter. Without each one of you this book would not be possible. Thank you, thank you, and thank you!

INTRODUCTION

When listening to and/or taking someone's advice I feel it's important to understand where his or her knowledge comes from in order to be confident with the information offered. My knowledge comes from trial and error, from years of tears and laughter. From life! Sharing challenging times of my life has never been easy and I will only relate events that demonstrate my knowledge and life lessons. I've faced many types of challenges, and at times I'm amazed I'm still here. I believe a major reason for my survival is my unwavering belief that I did not come to earth to suffer, but to learn, to grow mentally, spiritually, and to be happy! Still, there were times when I wondered, "Why me?" Then I wondered, "Why not me?" Perhaps what I was going through had little to do with me, but it greatly affected other lives. Maybe I would be their teacher.

Because of this belief, it is my intention to use my experiences to help you realize how truly remarkable you are, to help you discover your inner strength, and to offer suggestions on how to build a brighter future.

The journey to write this book began after speaking with a complete stranger. She opened my eyes to the importance of sharing my story and knowledge. This concept was foreign; my worries were for me alone, never to be discussed. I believed sharing my journey and knowledge through the pages of my first book, *Me, Myself and Eye, The Realities of Living With a Prosthetic Eye*; would complete my task. I was mistaken. To reach my intended audience, it was necessary to attend book signings, which resulted in requests to speak. Through those events I discovered most people wanted to know how to find the positives in tough situations. These questions propelled me to share other parts of my story and knowledge through the pages of this book.

Any emotion, such as fear, that prevents you from pursuing a happier life can be disabling. Whether your disability is visible or invisible, every one of us has a handicap. It may be a slight disability that's easy to live with or a major condition that affects every aspect of our lives.

Any type of loss will generate a stage of the grieving process, from shock, denial, anger, bargaining, depression, guilt to acceptance. However, the part of this process that seems to constantly weave in and out of our lives is periods of deep sadness and/or depression.

This book is divided into sections sharing stories, lessons, tips, exercises, and related information. It is intended to help you discover ways to free yourself from the grips of negativity to build inner peace and joy. Each section can stand on its own and I invite you to use what serves you best and leave the rest. What may not have seemed relevant yesterday may be just what you need today. Visit these pages often and smile. Congratulations, you're on your way to discovering ways to create a happier life.

Cynthia L. De Boer

Section One

MY JOURNEY AND THE NEED TO LIVE IN THE POSITIVE

MEDICAL CHALLENGES

I was born in 1960 with birth defects. By the time I was six-years-old I had undergone two open-heart surgeries, the first one at two weeks of age, three eye surgeries, and I had been on a ventilator. I also flat-lined three times and had even been given Last Rites on one of those occasions. My young parents were told I would be blind, retarded, and never reach the age of sixteen. They were also warned that a third birth defect might surface as they often came in threes.

The definitive reason for my defects was never proven; the possibility that my mother contracted German measles during her pregnancy was only a guess. It was dismissed, as she never exhibited any signs of the illness.

Very early on, with all the sad looks and concerned faces I saw in my world, I decided to put on that brave little soldier hat. No one was ever going to worry about me and my stubborn determination was going to make sure I proved every doctor wrong! Being headstrong enabled me not only to survive but also thrive.

My mother always commented that I was never a kid. I believe facing death at an early age matures you far beyond your years. Life also taught me that there are no coincidences; the universe is not that lazy. Events and patterns fall into line and grant us opportunities to become stronger mentally, emotionally, and spiritually. Life has never been easy; I always tried to look at the glass as half full—even if it was a little murky.

Through the years the troubles in my life became my characters' problems. Writing served me well. It offered me the chance to explore options for hope, garner a bit of compassion for my characters and myself, and not bother those who cared for me.

I was always an excellent student and although my vision was limited, by all accounts, my life was fairly normal. I triumphantly reached the age of sixteen, confident that I succeeded at beating the odds and achieved the ultimate goal. Life was good and I flourished. Nothing could possibly go wrong—or so I thought!

PHYSICAL LOSS

"At seventeen, I waited for a very special fitting. This was not for a formal dress to wear to a high school prom, but for an eye. I pretended it was an ordinary thing; something one does every day. Secretly, I was terrified!"

The above paragraph is the first one of my book, *Me, Myself and Eye, The Realities of Living With A Prosthetic Eye*. Me, Myself and Eye is the blending and acceptance of ME, the physical body, MYSELF, the emotional mind and EYE, the prosthesis … into a complete and healthy being.

In that book I shared my eye loss and what I discovered along the way. The book covers: the grieving process of loss; personal perceptions of self; how others may view you; instructions on care, the techniques to camouflage your prosthesis, how glasses can help or hinder the appearance of your eye; and the phantom phenomenon.

From the age of seventeen to twenty-eight I learned about my disability and grew in confidence and self-reliance. To most people, my disability was invisible. If a difference was noticed from one eye to another, people assumed my left eye was just lazy. They never guessed I was blind in that eye, much less that it was a prosthesis. Life and my search continued to discover more ways to live in a positive state of mind.

ROUGH RELATIONSHIPS

As the years ticked by, I experienced two horribly abusive relationships. They were years apart; the first was mentally and physically hurtful and the second was emotionally abusive. The descent from what I believed to be two distinct but loving partnerships into my subservient and oppressed roles was extremely difficult to understand. Each connection began so lovingly, but before long my two Mr.

Rights turned from Dr. Jekylls to Mr. Hyde. I honestly didn't recognize these two men. Happily ever after did not exist in my world.

For those who have never been in this type of partnership, it seems impossible that I or anyone else would allow ourselves to live in this environment. First of all, I couldn't grasp how anyone who loved me could treat me in such a harmful manner. It began with criticizing the little things I didn't do quite right and then progressed to outright insults. Sometimes I received an apology—laced with the fact that it was my fault for upsetting them. Before long the emotional abuse escalated to physical abuse. I felt it must be my fault because they had been so wonderful in the beginning. How could it possibly be them? After all, they constantly informed me that everything was my fault. I plummeted to feeling totally useless. It didn't matter what I did or didn't do, it was never good enough—I wasn't good enough!

When I partnered with others, I wanted to help them succeed in every area of their lives and since there's only so much time in the day, my hopes and dreams were soon smothered beneath theirs. I effectively placed myself below them, thereby allowing them to take control of every part of my life. My life was no longer my own; I existed to serve them. Because I cared about them and their lives I naively thought they would feel the same way—this was not the case. Going out of my way to do special things for them seemed to be appreciated at the start but soon these gestures were expected and taken for granted. The more I tried, the less it mattered.

My days grew dark as my role as their servant increased. My life spiraled down until there wasn't much of me remaining! I felt detached from reality and believed no one could possibly understand my situation—a situation I undeniably had a hand in creating. There were days when I struggled to see even one positive thing in my world. I was often relieved when the day came to a close; another empty day done. But then I fretted about what sadness the following day would hold. Even my sleep was poisoned with negativity; dreams made no sense and unimaginable nightmares infected my mind.

Gratefully, these dark days did not pass without merit, because as I searched for peace, I realized my strength and my ability to overcome any hardship. My understanding of the importance to analyze everything that transpired grew. I increased my ability to see patterns in behavior, to listen to voice intonation, to observe body language and sudden changes in attitude as well as step outside my feelings in order to be objective. These tools allowed me to survey both of these toxic relationships, giving me the strength to leave. It was my only option if I was to survive!

It took time and effort to plan my safe departures and even more time to regain control of my life, but it was worth it. No matter how my partners viewed me, I valued myself. I was important and deserved to be happy, to fulfill my dreams. My open, loving heart was a blessing, one worthy of protection.

Trust and respect must be earned, not given freely. No matter how many days we live under the veil of depression, we can rise up to a new brighter day. If we search for it, the light of hope will shine through lifting our hearts, minds, and spirits!

ROUND THREE BEGINS

At the age of thirty-seven I found my soul mate and less than a year and a half later, we were married. My beautiful daughter, the blessing from my first marriage, was grown and out in the world. I became stepmother to the three children from my husband's previous marriage who lived with us. We suffered the normal and sometimes not-so-normal growing pains of blended families, but for the most part we were happy.

Managing an appraisal and home inspection company was a rewarding career for me and my husband worked helping his family's business. With our financial and personal futures bright, we purchased a home.

Soon thereafter my husband was offered a new job with set hours and our lives took on a normal schedule. Then sadly, when my company downsized, my job ended. Determined to succeed, I quickly developed, owned, and operated an organizational consulting and cleaning business. It grew quite nicely; our financial rough patch seemed to be over.

TROUBLE, TROUBLE EVERYWHERE

The two years since our wedding brought many changes. Thankfully, they were all things we quickly adjusted to; that is, until my body began to betray me!

The vision in my right eye began exhibiting symptoms of Fuchs' Dystrophy, a corneal disease that had affected my left eye at the age of eleven. Blisters began forming on the front of my right eye. The pain was intense, causing uncontrollable tearing. When my eyelid opened or closed it rubbed over the open raw blisters. As the disease progresses the blisters stop erupting and the cornea begins to thicken. This happens as the cells of the cornea start to fail and do not release the water our bodies naturally secrete.

As the cornea thickened my vision became cloudier. It was like looking across a steamy shower; the more steam the less I saw. I refer to this as Fog Vision. In these early stages, the occurrences were sporadic and there was never a warning as to when they would take place. Sometimes my vision would decrease to the point that driving home from an appointment was impossible. At times I would sit and wait for hours hoping my sight would clear enough to return home safely. Soon the condition was constant and my vision decreased to 20/300.

As a point of reference, 20/200 is legally blind. The term legally blind doesn't necessarily mean totally without sight. In simple terms it means what people with 20/20 vision can see at two hundred feet a legally blind person can only see at twenty feet. Visually impaired might be a more apt description but whatever name you give it, it transforms every aspect of your life.

A corneal transplant is the only option for this corneal disease. But transplants do not last and usually three are the limit because of the fact that eye tissue diminishes with each surgery. Because of the risks, I opted to wait on the transplant. My work ended and debt increased.

My body also began to betray me. The most troubling of my symptoms was when occasionally my heart would beat erratically. I was used to this because of my mitral-valve prolapse but these episodes were more intense. Memories of my heart surgeries came flooding back. The possibility of another heart issue—much less another surgery—polluted my mind with fear.

Other symptoms included my entire left side feeling quite strange; it would go numb and I would fall as my leg gave way. There were also times when my face felt as if there was a hair on it or that someone was pulling it downward. Multiple sporadic and strange sensations emerged without warning. Additionally, I couldn't breathe through my left nostril and was frequently nauseous. I tried to dismiss the bulk of my physical problems to the stress caused by my decreased vision. This was my way of dealing with these new unknowns. Unfortunately, they soon became too much to ignore, resulting in more doctor visits, tests, and financial hardship.

An EKG and echocardiogram were performed on my heart; thankfully, my lifelong mitral-valve prolapse was the only thing detected for my erratic heartbeat. Reasons for my other symptoms were still undetermined and becoming worse.

The next test was a CAT scan of my head to determine if a cyst was blocking the air from my left nostril. During the test, the technician asked if I had recently been hit in the head. Because that hadn't occurred, it was indeed, a very odd question. The tech dismissed it as if it was nothing, but I was not convinced!

A phone call the following day verified my skepticism and turned my world upside down—again. It was late in the afternoon and I was home alone; the kids were at school, and my husband was at work. It went something like this:

"Hello," I answered.

"Hello, Cynthia, the doctor wants you to go in for an MRI as soon as possible because the CAT scan showed several brain tumors and there is also a cyst in your left nostril. Your blood workup showed … and your urinalysis showed …"

Quite frankly, receiving this type of news was overwhelming, much less to hear it over the phone as if reporting the local weather forecast. After she said "several brain tumors," my capacity to comprehend anything else was zero. I was in shock! My mind exploded in terror! How could this be? The only thing I'd ever heard about brain tumors was to get your affairs in order and plan to say goodbye to everyone and everything in this world.

I couldn't believe it. It must be a mistake. How could anyone be so cavalier to give such news over the phone? It must be a horrible joke. No one could be that unfeeling. No explanation, no information, just get an MRI!

I desperately wanted to pick up my CAT scans and report at the hospital; proof was necessary as soon as possible. Since I was unable to drive I would have to phone my husband. I asked him to come home immediately as there was something we needed to discuss. There was absolutely no way I could relay the news over the phone.

My words cracked as I shared the news. The look on his face was just as shocked as I imagined mine was. I had believed going blind was the worst thing that could happen, but now I was facing the genuine possibility of death. This sort of thing happened on soap operas—certainly not in real life!

We retrieved the report and with magnifying glass in hand I raced to the final paragraph, the Findings Section. It stated there were three epidermoid tumors/cysts on the right side of my brain. Thankfully, they were benign; still, surgery would be necessary. Research revealed that a person is born with these types of tumors, hence, my third birth defect. The doctors' predictions in this case were unfortunately correct. Apparently, it takes until the approximate age of forty before they grow large enough to become problematic.

Epidermoids are like egg yolks of acid and if they rupture they cause significant damage. Before surgery could be performed, one tumor did rupture and the corrosive substance ate through the dura layer that surrounds my brain. When it occurred I literally believed I was going to die. It affected my entire body and the feelings were so complex and strange it's quite difficult to fully explain.

For the most part, surgery was a success. The acid-like substance from the ruptured tumor was flushed out and a second tumor was removed intact. The third was left behind because of its location deep in a fissure of the brain. Removing it would have caused more harm than good. Some residual effects remain, but thankfully, I never suffered from seizures before or after the surgery. Most importantly, I was grateful and happy to be alive!

Then trouble reared its ugly head in a new direction. Another fateful phone call relayed tragic news. My mother was diagnosed with terminal cancer. It seemed peace for any extended period of time was not to be. Because I wasn't working, I accompanied my mom to doctor appointments, chemo and radiation treatments. My head was partially shaved and my blind cane was in hand; nonetheless, my troubles seemed minuscule compared to what my mother and the other patients were dealing with. Seeing the sickness and listening to their hardships was heart-wrenching. The amazing and often unbelievable side was the courage, strength, and positive attitudes many patients exhibited. True heroes, each and every one!

My mother's way of dealing with her disease was to tell my brother, sister, daughter, and father what she wanted them to believe. I'm sure they were the same things she, too, wanted desperately to believe. Unfortunately, this left me as the messenger of the awful reality: my mother's life was coming to an end. When family members would question the differences between my reports and what they were told by my mother, many became furious with me. Even though I understood venting their anger toward me was easier than accepting my mother's impending death, it was horrible to be on the receiving end of such pain. The truth of the matter was I was hurting, too. My anger built as there wasn't a thing I could do to stop their pain or save my mother. It was all out of my control, allowing fear to take over. One moment I was crying because I was losing her and the next minute I was furious because she hadn't stopped smoking decades earlier after being diagnosed with the early signs of emphysema.

Wrestling with these multiple and often conflicting feelings turned life into an endless nightmare. Emotions darted in and out of my mind, attacking me; fear, anger, frustration, helplessness, confusion, and even shame were all parts of this severe grieving process. I was grieving my mother before she died and felt guilty for doing that. Every holiday was made even more special, every event done with a bit more enthusiasm because it could be her last. We all tried our best, knowing how cheated and hurt we felt. It was a very traumatic time of our lives.

A terminal diagnosis creates this and yes, it gives one the time to get one's affairs in order and truly appreciate someone before they're gone. However, it is also a time filled with the feeling of being completely powerless and the realization that we don't control our lives no matter how hard we try to convince ourselves otherwise. Control over life and death is an illusion. Our time here is fleeting and every minute is precious and should be treasured.

Financially, my medical bills continued to mount and the reality that we may lose our home weighed heavy. Home life was difficult as my husband and I tried to maintain as much normalcy as possible for all our kids and families. I felt pretty inadequate in every role of my life because of my decreased vision. No matter how many times I recited my list of blessings or tried to smile at anything positive, I found myself crying over the littlest things. Depression invaded every cell of my being, becoming unbearable.

I desperately needed help and forced myself to seek it out. This search for assistance led me to a new way to view my stress, allowing me to move forward, to create a more positive life. I've named this new way The Stress Cup, shared later in these pages!

> "So often times it happens that we live our lives in chains and we never even know we have the key."
> *Lyrics from "Already Gone," a 1976 song by The Eagles*

ON TO YOUR JOURNEY

I am a student of life and a product of my experiences: good, bad, or indifferent. Because of this, I hope sharing some of the most difficult times of my life enables you to understand that we all face varied and at times, insurmountable odds. Each of us will handle our struggles differently. Some may need to speak with a friend or professional to work things out while others may require medication to ease troubled times. Simply said, when the world seems to conspire against us we need to be brave. Brave enough to ask for help because it takes courage to build a better life. Every step forward, no matter how insignificant it may seem, will be transformative.

Everything takes time and time is a commodity we can't replace. It follows, then, that time should not be wasted, and every moment created in happiness will build a more blissful life. Continuing to add joy will create hope and from hope you will be able to discover ways to make it through and/or solve life's challenges. Read on, customize, and implement the ideas and tips that appeal to you; leave the rest and reread as often as you desire. What you may find helpful today may be different tomorrow. This book is a gift of positives to you.

"We know what we are but know not what we may be."
~ William Shakespeare

Section Two

TEACHABLE MOMENTS

THE STRESS CUP

Facing multiple problems and constantly existing in a state of stress overload, I needed help and turned to my doctor. Still, I was opposed to using anti-depressants because of the possible interactions with my other medications. My lifelong tenacious grit to overcome whatever life threw at me was also at the forefront of my mind. Learning to deal with my circumstances without medical intervention was a necessity for me. I am not against the use of medication; it just wasn't right for me at that moment in time. Every person should choose a treatment plan they are comfortable with, one designed for their specific needs.

As I was not in favor of medical intervention I hoped my physician would have another idea; thankfully, he did. His explanation was a variation of the following, which I adapted and named, *The Stress Cup*. Begin by viewing everything causing you stress, large and small, as extremely hot black coffee. When your cup is full to the brim and even one tiny drop is added, a large amount of liquid will slosh over the sides. The release of this steaming fluid represents stress overload and explains why, when one minor thing occurs, we emotionally break down. Just as the cup's capacity is at its limit, unable to take in one additional tiny drop, our bodies can't handle one more thing, no matter how minute.

We can help ourselves by analyzing every item causing sadness or stress. Obviously, there will be major things you cannot eliminate but what about the small irritants in your daily life? Observe what they are and adopt ways to change or remove them completely.

For instance: because of my minimal sight I was constantly breaking clear glass items, from drinking glasses to bowls and knick-knacks. Every break would result in me getting angry at my condition and myself. This was coupled with the frequent occurrences of being cut by invisible shards of glass as I attempted to clean up the mess. My solution: give away clear items and use the colored things we already owned. Gifting treasured knick-knacks to those who would appreciate them and donating other items to the less fortunate was satisfying. My inability to see these clear items offered me an opportunity to do something pleasant for someone else.

Downsizing my wardrobe was helpful, too. When traveling I chose simple yet interchangeable clothing. I simply applied the same technique to my entire wardrobe. What remained were the colors I loved and that worked well together. No matter what was pulled from my wardrobe I was confident with my appearance. It also freed up space, making my clothes more accessible. Getting dressed in the morning was a delight and my day began with confidence instead of frustration. Once again, I donated unwanted items, making it a definite Win, Win situation.

Here's another dilemma and its solution: Because I always carried a purse, adding my cane meant not having a free hand. This was extremely aggravating because I couldn't catch myself if I tripped or wanted to pick up something. My solution was to exchange my purse for a backpack, fanny pack, or a cross-shoulder bag allowing me the needed free hand.

And finally, a coffee shop problem solved: Every sip meant searching for the hole in the top of the plastic lid on the to-go coffee cup. I devised this trick to fix that irritation. First, find the seam on the cup itself and align it on the right or left side of the cup. The placement doesn't matter, as long as you know where it is. Next, remove the lid and locate the drink hole by feel and center it toward you. After that, you'll always know where the opening is by casually feeling the seam. It works great, making an otherwise frustrating trip to a coffee shop a joyful outing without hunting.

Even small alterations today can have an immediate, transformative impact on your life. These seemingly trivial changes allowed my emotional breakdowns to occur less frequently. Each small success lightened my mood, freeing room for hope to develop. Solutions for improving our financial and personal situations also began to surface. I effectively emptied some of my stress from my cup, and you can, too.

"Changes call for innovation, and innovation leads to progress."
~ *Li Kequang*

DISABILITIES VS. HANDICAPS

Disability and handicap are often used interchangeably; let's examine their true meanings.

Webster's Dictionary defines a disability as: a physical, mental, cognitive, or developmental condition that impairs, interferes with, or limits a person's ability to engage in certain tasks or actions or participate in typical daily activities and interactions. A handicap, however, is defined as an *added advantage or disadvantage*.

You can decide how to view your handicap or disability and most importantly, how you feel about it! Do your feelings serve you in a healthy manner or are they making you unhappy, stressed-out or depressed? Any feeling you cannot control can become a disability. Fear is a very powerful emotion and can often stop us from pursuing our dreams.

In my case, I looked for the positives my limited sight offered. I found that my decreased vision taught me to appreciate the senses I do have, as well as my remaining sight. The loss made me pay even closer attention to a person's body language and voice intonation. The emotion attached to every word is often more important than the word itself. I listened to how every word was spoken. For instance, saying, "I love you" with a negative tone can transform the statement into an insult.

The lavish feel of a velvety soft blanket, the glorious sound of a chorus, the enticing smell of cinnamon, the rich taste of chocolate, and the ability to move are simply magical to me. Without my vision loss I may have never gained a genuine appreciation for those miraculous things. Sadly, many people take these incredible gifts for granted.

Having a disability does not make you less of a person; it makes you more of a human being.

Disabilities change our worlds; sometimes it becomes quieter with the loss of hearing, or it may appear smaller because of limited sight or a complete loss of vision. It might seem to be a world of unending barriers for those with mobility issues.

One of the things they all have in common is the need to slow down because it simply takes longer to accomplish most things. We need to *Embrace the Slower Pace!* Moving slower can be frustrating in this hurry-up world, but the rewards are great. Some refer to it as becoming Zen-like. It's the act of focusing all our energy and thoughts on one thing, no matter what it is. From washing a dish to getting from one point to another, every movement and task becomes the most important thing in that moment.

Many times while we are working on the first task of the day we find ourselves thinking about the tenth item on our list. Then, once we arrive at number ten we start wondering if we actually accomplished the third and fourth things earlier in the day. Our day becomes one nonstop blur of events with no real attention or appreciation for any single thing we've accomplished. By not giving our undivided attention to the current project we rob ourselves of that particular experience, leaving our days filled with empty and mind-numbing chores — just the same old same old — human hamsters on a wheel going nowhere. Wouldn't it be better to truly experience every moment, finding joy in even the most mundane task? While washing a dish, feel the silkiness of the water and look at the pattern of each dish and pan. Think about what meal was prepared or eaten off each dish. Perhaps the conversations that developed over a meal. When sorting clothing, feel grateful for the fact that you have clothes and the comfort and security they bring. While fueling your automobile be grateful for your transportation. If you think about everything in your life and how each item improves or adds to your existence, it is impossible to ignore the positives that surround you.

In addition, performing two tasks simultaneously has been proven to be impossible; therefore, multitasking cannot truly exist. One of the two tasks will suffer. For example, when you try to brush your hair and your teeth at the same time, you'll find one hand stops as you concentrate on the other task. The result is neither one is accomplished well. Once you realize there is no real multitasking your life will simplify and become much more efficient. Relish each moment, one second at a time.

Once again, smiling at the simple pleasures life has to offer and feeling grateful for every blessing, no matter how small, will be delightful!

> "What great thing would you attempt if you knew you could not fail?"
> ~ **Robert H. Schuller**

EXCUSES VS. ALLOWANCES

As we have discussed, words have power because they elicit feelings. Learning to choose your words wisely will change a negative to a positive. An excuse is an apology. An allowance is a charitable view of somebody or something taking circumstances into account.

Take a look at these examples:
1. "Excuse me, I can't get through with my wheelchair."
2. "I need a bit more room; please allow me to pass.

In sentence one you're asking for forgiveness; in sentence two you're asking for an allowance. I don't know about you but I feel my disability doesn't need to be forgiven. Certain allowances just need to be set in place.

I believe it's important to stop making excuses and blaming our handicap for our changing abilities and merely examine ways to make allowances for them. Adapting your environment to fit your disability makes life easier and the tiniest of things can be quite helpful. Your disability is not something to apologize for; it's simply a different way of living and we should allow ourselves the ability to create our new world.

Here's a simple example: If someone changes professions from construction worker to salesman, his or her wardrobe has to adapt to fit the new position. A different job will most likely include learning other skills, buying, storing and caring for needed business attire, a new work location and schedule, and perhaps even switching from a truck to a four-door car for transporting potential clients. Tightening one's financial belt until things start rolling is another factor to consider. Allowances have to be made for each change.

With change comes apprehension as we let go of old habits and possessions. Still, we do what's needed in hopes of creating a better life. Transforming our world to allow for the needs of our disability holds as much merit as adjusting our lives for a new profession. We all deserve to live in comfort and happiness. A disability is not a punishment — it's a challenge!

"If it doesn't Challenge you, it doesn't Change you."
~ *Fred DeVito*

WE HAVE A DISABILITY

While I was speaking with a low-vision group a woman I will call Barb and her husband sat together holding hands. When the time came to ask questions, she began with a statement, "We have a disability and I was wondering how you adjusted to your new life?"

Barb didn't realize the truth and power of her statement. If we are blessed with a partner, family or close friends, they all carry the effects of our personal disability. The people in our lives can be a great comfort if we let them in. We can do this by stating the facts, letting them know what we can and can't do, what needs to be altered to adapt to our new life, and what allowances they can make to assist in this transition.

The flip side of this is to understand that they, too, will be going through the grieving process and will also be weaving in and out of depression. You have changed; therefore, your way of life and your relationships will also change. It's as difficult for them as it is for you. This is most likely new territory for them, too. The dilemma of what to say or ask us is extremely hard. If we're in a good mood they may not want to ask how we are for fear of bringing us down; if we're down, they don't want to ask because they worry they might really depress us. This often means they don't ask at any time, because when is the right time? They're as emotionally fragile as we are and that's when we, the disabled person, needs to take the first step and open a line of dialogue.

In Barb's case, she was upset with her new life and found herself snapping at her husband when things weren't the way they used to be. At times he snapped back, too. Adjustments and allowances needed to be made to accept their current life. When stressful times occurred, I advised them to stop, take a few breaths, count to ten, and think about why they were upset. Chances are they weren't angry with the each other, they were upset with the issue they were currently facing.

The acronym S.T.O.P. is used in survival situations and it's also beneficial at these times. It stands for Stop, Think, Observe, and Plan. **S**top and take a few deep breaths to calm down. **T**hink about the situation or problem and **O**bserve how it's currently being handled, along with some possible alternatives. Then **P**lan a fresh course of action. This plan may include sharing each person's frustrations, ideas, or options to manage things more effectively. It may be a time when one or the other party needs to relinquish the chore or duty to the other. It may also be a matter of one person taking the time to learn how to complete the task in the manner the other person prefers.

Here are a few examples: After helping me fold the laundry, my husband left the room feeling proud of his contribution. I was angry with him because his way was different from mine. My irritation caused me to thrash the clothes about, refolding them as tears ran down my face. When I stopped and thought about the real reason I was upset, which was my inability to do all I used to, I realized I was angry with myself, with my disability. Observing how my husband folded the laundry allowed me to develop a plan. I sat down with him and thanked him for assisting me, shared my feelings, and asked if he would mind folding the laundry the way I preferred. He happily agreed, another small reason I love him dearly. He understood and helped me maintain control of this small thing. With a moment of bonding one small irritant was transformed into an accomplishment, bringing us even closer.

 The second example concerns my losing the ability to drive at the age of forty. It was extremely difficult for me and if I'm totally honest, I still miss the freedom and independence driving a vehicle provided me.

Most often I viewed other drivers and their lack of attention as a form of entertainment, though I'm not saying there weren't times of irritation. But the majority of the time I realized they probably didn't even know my vehicle existed. They were too wrapped up in their own lives and the lists of things they wanted to accomplish.

I've always been a tomboy and I enjoyed working on my own car. I loved driving and the feel of the open road as the tires hugged the asphalt, the thrill of the screech of laying rubber as I revved the engine, released the brake, and popped the clutch. There's truly nothing like the roar of an engine as the sound vibrates off the walls of a tunnel late at night when no one else is on the road. To see the flash of sparks from my side pipes and feel the power and excitement of racing through the tunnel was thrilling. The knowledge that I was partly responsible for it gave me such a feeling of being in control. All of that was lost; being a passenger pales in comparison to being behind the wheel.

I enjoyed performing chores and going places on my own. Unfortunately, once the luxury of driving was gone it became a necessity to plan my trips in advance. Not wanting to be a burden to my driver, I would prepare a list of places and items needed. Someone would drive me to each location and I would race through gathering only what was needed. Of course, my husband and anyone else in the role of my driver caught on right away and urged me to slow down. They said they felt there wasn't anything they could do to change my disability but helping me allowed them to feel useful. My husband also commented that he liked sharing the chores with me.

There is no doubt that disabilities change our lives. It's normal to miss lost abilities but in order to accept our lives as they are we need to cherish our memories and find new joys and ways to enrich our lives.

There are a few upsides to losing the ability to drive. The need to plan your outings will encourage you to be more organized and conscious of your routes. You may value your time a bit more because of spending it with another. This time together will offer the opportunity to share new experiences. It also gives your driver the pride that comes from feeling useful. Essentially, they are not only gifting the use of their vehicle to you, they are gifting you an irreplaceable commodity, their time. Nothing could be more precious!

> "Most of us have far more courage than we ever dreamed we possessed."
> ~ *Dale Carnegie*

WHY AM I EXTREMELY EXHAUSTED?

By noon on most days I was exhausted mentally and physically. This added to my depression, as I certainly wasn't the same energetic person from my past. My husband often commented that I had two speeds, full on and off. Sadly, off now occurred at noon. Becoming legally blind took a toll. Everything in my world became extremely challenging; I didn't want to be seen as disabled. I was sick of being tired and having to work so hard to do virtually everything I used to do with ease.

I decided to speak to a therapist specializing in working with the blind. I will call her Jane. We met at a local library; she was already there when I arrived and watched as I walked toward her. After brief introductions our conversation went like this.

She began, "Why are you just holding your cane and not using it?"

The question caught me off guard, but after a moment I answered, "Because there are definite areas of light and dark colors from the furniture to the flooring. I can see well enough to maneuver around things. And if a place is familiar I remember the floor plan making the use of my cane unnecessary."

She tilted her head, studying my face as she responded, "You know that's not all; it's because you don't want to be disabled or have others view you as such. Isn't that true?"

My words erupted from my lips with anger, "Yes, it's hard because I've always been so independent and I never wanted anyone to feel sorry for me or treat me differently. The moment people notice my cane they avoid me, begin speaking loudly, or talk to me as if I'm ignorant. I'm not deaf and I haven't lost the ability to think. I'm still the same person!" This was the first time I voiced my frustration and saying those words out loud caused a flood of emotion. I blinked my eyes as I fought back the tears.

Jane gently patted my hand. "I understand your feelings and coming to grips with your disability is a difficult process, but it's necessary to move forward. Now that we have that out of the way, what did you want to discuss with me?"

My tension eased and my words softened. "I'm exhausted by noon and want to know what I can do about it."

She replied with a question, "Are there any steps at your home?"

I didn't understand how that would possibly matter but casually answered, "Yes, there are six from the sidewalk to the front yard, ten inside to the basement and four from the back door to the backyard.

Jane smiled and asked, "Who else in your family knows this?"

In fact, no one else did, because it wasn't necessary. In a flash, they saw what they needed to know. The therapist explained that my necessity to count every step and memorize places a perfectly sighted person could instantly see used much more energy. Logically, wearing out earlier in the day was a natural occurrence, which would diminish as I adjusted to this new way of life. It was quite a revelation. I had begun counting steps as a way of preventing falls. Counting became second nature and I never gave it a thought. With this new insight I was confident the other trying things in my new world would soon become second nature, too.

This additional use of energy applies to anyone with any sort of disability. If you're hearing impaired, you will concentrate and rely on what you see. No matter if you're in a powered or manual wheelchair, your upper body and arms will be in higher demand to allow you to move. If you've lost of a limb or have another type of impairment, you will make up the difference in ability by using another sense or part of your body. If you've lost complete control of your body, having to depend on others may drain your emotional and mental reserves. Having a learning disability, mental, or emotional problem will also be demanding. We may need to write or record more things, retrace steps or analyze everything and every thought. No matter what the disability, compensating for it requires more energy.

As my body and mind adapted to the new demands my stamina rose and becoming tired early in the day decreased. I adjusted and learned to cope with my new world. Most people I've talked with have experienced the same thing, no matter how severe their disability. What seemed quite demanding in the beginning soon became a normal part of their lives. Just like counting steps became second nature, so did many other things, all accomplished without a thought.

Be patient with yourself; anything worthwhile takes time. You also need to remember your friends and family are adjusting to your new life, too. Be patient with them as well.

"We humans have lost the wisdom of genuinely resting and relaxing. We worry too much. We don't allow our bodies to heal, and we don't allow our minds and hearts to heal."
~ *Nhat Hahn*

MY FATHER'S BED

After my mother passed away from cancer, my father, husband, and I moved in together. It was especially difficult for my father as he met my mom when they were teenagers. My father went from his parents' house to sharing a home with my mother and other than a few trips apart, they were never without one another. Her death altered my father's life in every conceivable way.

One afternoon my husband stepped into my father's room while I was making the bed. We began chatting and he jumped in to complete the task. Before long he was making the bed the way we made ours. When I stopped him, he commented that our way was the way it should be done. I explained that making the bed in the fashion Dad preferred was a small thing he could control, just as he controlled the design and elements in his room. Getting into a bed prepared exactly as one prefers is a relaxing way to end the day; if it's not how we prefer, relaxation can quickly turn into aggravation.

In my father's case, there wasn't anything he could do to save my mother; therefore, feelings of helplessness and not being in control took over. Changing or controlling the little things in our lives may seem inconsequential; however, small things multiply into a more peaceful existence.

> "Try to be a rainbow in someone's cloud."
> ~ *Maya Angelou*

THE BORING BODY

What is perfection and who decides? Is it society, the latest famous star, the magazines that tell women there's always something we can do to improve virtually every aspect of ourselves and our lives? The word 'perfect' is defined as faultless, flawless, ideal, and unspoiled. But isn't that objective? We say things like, "Robert is perfect for Susan." "Susan found the perfect job, house, babysitter, diet, and so on…" The perfect things Susan fills her life with would not be perfect for someone else, so how can they possibly be referred to as perfect? The answer is really quite simple: perfection, like beauty, is in the eye of the beholder and it's different for everyone. Indeed, we are all perfect just as we are.

Men don't seem to be as inundated with this message to the extent that women are and many regard scars and black eyes as badges of honor. My stepson is a fine example of that. He had a mountain bike accident when he was in high school and required stitches in his knee. He was so excited that he was a blood donor on Bootleg Canyon. He said triumphantly, "It was epic! You should have seen it! The guys couldn't believe it!" To top that off, he placed his hospital armband and stitches in a plastic bag and proudly displayed it in his room. He also showed off his scar and told the story behind it whenever he had the chance. It was wonderful to see his pride and joy.

Most women, on the other hand, strive for flawless; scars are to be erased, not revealed. Every year millions of women strive to achieve society's ever-changing idea of perfection. I've witnessed the back and forth from plucked skinny eyebrows to untouched thick lush eyebrows. Long hair is cut to various lengths and dyed from one color, to another, then left to grow long again. Hair curled one year and straightened the next. Clothing styles transform from one extreme to another as well as every season's perfect color used on every perfect product imaginable.

The fear of not being good enough is a great motivator and fear is an advertiser's greatest tool or how I view it — weapon! This weapon is fueled by the greed of the almighty dollar.

Advertisers want to make money and fear motivates consumers to purchase.

Of course, not all advertisers practice these tactics and there are many valuable products and services. To make logical buying decisions, one must remove the emotion of fear and investigate the claims or implied results. Are they realistic? As we know, time is a commodity we can't replace and we need to consider how much time a new possession will take from our lives. How many hours of work will it take to pay and care for the item? Is it truly worth our time? Will the product or service assist us or merely remove money from our wallet? Would our life improve with the purchase and what are the responsibilities associated with ownership? Is it right for us?

Here's a simple example: "Joan, I realize dark maroon is this season's perfect lip color, but it certainly doesn't mean it's the best choice for your beautiful pale skin, and it may overshadow your gorgeous blue eyes, too." A statement like this allows Joan to understand that she has a lot to offer and this season's perfect lip color may not be the right for her. It may not be right for her, not the other way around! The compassion shown to friends should be extended to yourself! Look for your positive attributes and make the most of them. Who knows, tomorrow you may be America's idea of perfect. However — beware — it will not last; advertisers have bills to pay and that's impossible unless you keep buying!

My life has taken a fairly normal path with all the growing pains of desperately trying to fit into the perfect mold society has crafted for the American woman. And sadly, I must admit I knew all along it wasn't realistic. It's difficult to ignore the constant bombardment of the latest, greatest product, but peace comes from learning to be confident in your own skin. Thankfully, I have arrived at a time in my life where I understand that I have my faults like everyone else. I no longer feel the need to apologize for being me, or more likely, for who others believe I should be! I'm perfectly content in the knowledge that there is absolutely no possible way to please everyone, nor should I try.

No, I do not have a flawless body like the ones seen in most women's magazines; instead, I have a body flawed from surviving this world. Each imperfection tells a story and my body has a great deal to say. Every line is from a smile or a tear. My stretch marks are evidence that I've experienced the miracle of creating, carrying, and giving birth. And I must say, the miracle of life is worth a few stretch marks. My numerous scars show my strength and ability to endure. My body is the chart of my life and is absolute proof that it has been eventful and not a bit boring!

I'm perfectly unique — faults and all — just like everyone else and my imperfections are what make me a perfect human being. After all, imperfect can be read as I'm-perfect!

> "True contentment in one's self is a state of mind and not a commodity to be purchased."
> ~ *Cynthia L. De Boer*

HEALTHY RESPECT

During my rough relationships, I lost myself and thereby my self-respect. To recover it, I reviewed all my accomplishments and the important people in my life. This allowed me to recognize my worth and dignity and respect myself once again. It took time and effort, as everything worthwhile does. But when we arrive at the point in our lives when we can acknowledge our own value, it is the most rewarding gift we can bestow on ourselves.

Please understand, I'm not referring to conceit; I'm talking about a healthy respect for yourself and the life you've lived. Most of us believe we are no one special; just another human trying to make it through whatever life throws at us. But isn't that the point? Our individual trials and triumphs help mold us into who we are. We are products of our individual experiences and how we've responded to them.

When I was asked why I felt I was qualified to be an author and speaker as I wasn't anyone rich, famous, or held multiple degrees, my answer was simple. Yes, it's true, I wasn't born rich or famous. My degrees come from the school of life and from my varied work experiences. My certifications come from meeting and conquering difficult challenges and surviving them all to thrive on this planet. So why not share my journey and the hard-earned lessons life has awarded me with the world's majority of normal people like myself? Each of us is special to someone and our stories deserve to be shared to inspire, to teach, to be! We all go through periods of sadness and knowing others out there are experiencing the same thing will, at the very least, bring a small sense of comfort in the knowledge that we are not alone.

One definition for *hero* is a person, who in the opinion of others, has special achievements, abilities, or personal qualities and is regarded as a role model or ideal.

> "We relish news of our heroes, forgetting that we are extraordinary to someone too!"
> *~ Helen Hayes*

A SINGLE CRAYON

Long ago my husband and I hosted a youth group. It was quite a mixture of ages, races, and social standings. The kids went off in different directions only wanting to be with their friends. It seemed no one wanted to give anyone else a chance. In addition, most activities were designed for specific age groups making it difficult to find things everyone might enjoy.

I'm not sure how the 'One Color' idea came about, but we hoped it would help the group bond. Each child was asked to choose his or her favorite color from the box of crayons and instructed to draw a picture. Before long they began asking for other colors. Comments like, "I can't draw a flower with only pink," or "A car isn't just blue; what about the tires?"

Our reply, "Well, you chose your favorite color, why isn't that good enough?"

"Things aren't just one color," was the normal response.

As they sat waiting for additional colors we asked another question, "What is your favorite food?" Curiously cocking their heads, they answered. The responses were normal kid choices: mac and cheese, pizza, spaghetti, burgers, and hotdogs.

We proudly announced, "Okay, kids, from now on you will have only your favorite food for breakfast, lunch, snack time, and dinner. What do you all think of that?" Except for one little boy who absolutely adored pizza, everyone else thought his or her favorite food would become monotonous in no time at all.

We went on to explain that variety in all areas of our lives is desired, and at times, necessary. We continued to say the same applied to people. How dull the world would be if it were all clones, exact copies of one another. They began to look around the room, to truly see one another. This small step toward creating a more cohesive group made a huge difference. Each child in the group was able to realize the world needed individuality, a uniqueness that made everyone perfect in their own way!

> "Nature always wears the colors of the spirit."
> *~ Ralph Waldo Emerson*

WHAT'S IN THE HAT?

We continued to bring our group together with another activity. We asked the kids to write their three worst problems on a piece of paper. They weren't to be signed — just folded and placed in a large hat. We shook the hat and each child picked out a problem. My husband or I would read the paper and watch the children's reactions.

What an eye opener for those with trivial problems, such as wanting a new toy or a television in their bedroom. Those children gained a new respect for those with serious troubles, like a parent being out of work or an illness in the family. The less fortunate realized they were not alone by discovering others with serious problems. Even though no one knew whose problems were whose, a new respect for one another was apparent and bonds deepened.

The children also agreed they wouldn't want anyone else's problems. They were confident they could handle their troubles but could not imagine dealing with another child's problem.

Sharing our worries can bring us together, no matter our age, race, or social standing. We are all on this journey together; let's help one another along the way.

> "I am an old man and have known a great many troubles, but most of them never happened."
> ~ *Mark Twain*

WRAPPED IN LOVE

I would like to share more about the evening one of my brain tumors ruptured. It happened a few days before my scheduled surgery. My husband was at a meeting and the kids were out with friends. I was milling around the house tidying up when suddenly I became extremely dizzy; the right side of my head — where the tumors were located — hurt and felt hot on the inside. My heart began to race, my neck began to hurt, and my entire body felt strange. Every nerve ending seemed to be on high alert. My fear of passing out with no one knowing what happened or how to help weighed heavy. It would be at least an hour before anyone was expected home. Cautiously, I made my way to the couch to lie down. I quickly grabbed the phone off the end table and called my husband. I relayed my symptoms and asked him to come home immediately. I knew he was nearby and would arrive within minutes.

I didn't want to move because of the extreme dizziness, fearing any movement might cause me to pass out. If that happened I worried I wouldn't wake up. Exhaustion hit as my body tried to recover and I strained to stay awake. My head was pounding and continued to feel hot while the rest of my body was freezing.

My husband rushed in the door and said my skin appeared pale and gray. Because we had researched these epidermoid tumors, we knew they could rupture and the symptoms I was feeling matched the research. The only solution was to flush the infected area, which would not be possible until surgery. Since my symptoms seemed to be stabilizing and my heartbeat was returning to normal, we opted to wait a bit.

My body was still cold, so I asked my husband for a blanket. Instead of covering me with the afghan on the nearby chair, he raced to the bedroom and returned with a beautiful handmade quilt. He purchased it as a surprise to give to me at the hospital but felt I needed it right then. What a loving and thoughtful gift; his generosity brought tears of joy to my eyes. What an amazing man; my life was and is blessed by him each and every day.

I was comforted and warmed by the beautiful quilt and my symptoms eased. They never completely dissipated but I could function as I waited for surgery. The surgeon confirmed the rupture and reported the acid-like substance ate through a portion of the dura layer that surrounds my brain. He flushed it away and removed a second cyst. The third one was left in place as it was located far down in the fissure of the brain. Removing it would cause more damage than good. Because these types of tumors grow so slowly the doctor felt sure leaving it behind wouldn't cause problems for decades, if ever.

When I recall the night of the rupture, I remember being wrapped in love above all else. My husband's care minimized one of the most frightening experiences of my life. The gift of the quilt represents a treasured part of my life.

I share this story with you because the memories of a favorite blanket or item of clothing can transform even a tragic event into a time of comfort and love. Surround yourself with comfort. A velvety throw, afghan, or quilt in a favorite fabric or perhaps a gift from a special someone is always nice to have nearby. You may even want to toss items in the dryer for a few moments for added warmth. A warm fluffy towel after bathing is a welcome pleasure. The fabrics that touch our lives from furnishings to clothing affect our feelings. Choose what brings you a sense of well-being and joy.

> "Love is love's reward."
> *~ John Dryden*

BE THE DETECTIVE OF YOUR LIFE!

From a very young age, the elderly held my attention. They amazed me with their years of living, of experiencing things long since passed. When my family went camping, and my sister and brother would be off with their friends, I was at the edge of the lake talking to a mature person. Perhaps this was because I was trying to gain as much knowledge as I could while I raced through what I knew could possibly be a very short life.

The lake holds treasured memories of wonderfully gracious people. I would ask the elderly to tell me about their lives, the lessons they learned, the places they visited, the jobs they held, and anything else that came into my mind. The thought that I was being forward never entered my head and I was never turned down for a conversation. It seemed they genuinely wanted to share their journey and I was definitely an eager listener.

The knowledge I gained from these virtual strangers was wonderful. It taught me that everything and everyone has something to share. By not making snap decisions about a situation, thing, or person, but by truly analyzing all aspects, we open our minds to possibilities and fresh ideas.

An individual may be a fine example of someone to be admired and emulated or represent the exact opposite. Every person provides examples of traits we may choose to adopt or not. We can decide to be a kind person, someone to be respected, or someone others avoid because of our negativity.

Focusing on the positive traits of a person or item is a wonderful way to view the world, but it's also important to understand that sometimes the negatives far outweigh the positives. In those instances, these people and things should not have a place in our lives. Keep your best interests and safety in the forefront of your mind.

How a particular item is used will often dictate whether it's viewed as a positive or a negative thing. For example, a baseball bat can be used to play an enjoyable game or as a weapon to hurt someone. So, is a bat a good or bad thing? Both uses contain lessons and both examples can be turned around. What if the bat propels the ball into someone's head, resulting in a severe injury, or it isn't used as a weapon but to ward off an attack? The truth of the matter is — the bat is neither good nor bad! It's the person's use of the bat that becomes a positive or negative thing.

Knowing fire is hot and can burn us should never be ignored. However, the fact that heat can keep us warm and cook our food are uses we should focus on and be grateful for. No matter what we encounter, we benefit most when we understand the negatives but place all our energy and attention on the positives. This allows us to live in a hopeful and grateful state of mind. Hope and good thoughts draw in positive energy, which manifests into sincere feelings of happiness and in turn, will create a more positive world.

> "I don't focus on what I'm up against. I focus on my goals and I try to ignore the rest."
> ~ *Venus Williams*

PURPOSE TO PLAN/ MAP IT OUT

In order to be successful, the things we do need to be planned. Whenever making changes or beginning a new venture it's helpful to devise a system or map it out. One method is to create a list of all the needed supplies in order to formulate the steps necessary to start and complete the task.

The method I prefer is to map out everything. I use a large sheet of paper and write the goal or final objective in a large circle in the middle of the paper. From that lines are drawn out from the center with all the needed steps and supplies.

The following is a sample map: How to rearrange a kitchen for easy access. Draw a large circle with 'New Kitchen' written in the center of the page and the purpose for the project. Keeping the purpose in mind at all times will help you stay on track. From the center, lines are drawn out to headings such as Needed for Easy Access and Seldom Used, Items No Longer Needed, Items to Buy, and The Process Needed to Rearrange Items. List everything under their appropriate headings. The map is a great way to see everything in its proper place and it's easy to include everything and every step of the entire process on one large sheet of paper.

No matter what method you prefer, planning is the key to success at whatever task is before you. It also simplifies life. We wouldn't want to build a house without a set of plans, so why would we want to work on any project without a plan, much less build a life without one? Be aware, it's normal for plans to change and adapt as life takes us on a different course or new wants or needs arise. Still, without a plan we flounder with no concrete idea of how to proceed. If you truly desire success in anything—plan!

> "The Purpose is why we do things and the Plan brings the Purpose to life!"
> ~ *Cynthia L. De Boer*

CHANGE AND MAGNETISM

There are laws we live with and accept daily. Fire is hot, ice is cold, rocks are hard, and feathers are soft. In addition, the Law of Gravity is never questioned or doubted. Whatever is dropped from a high elevation will plummet to the ground.

And even though we logically know other laws are true, we ignore or refuse to use them. One law that is a true constant in life is change! Everything and everyone is constantly changing. However, when we find ourselves in a tough spot, we often forget that today's circumstances will not be tomorrow's.

The Law of Magnetism and the Law of Attraction are well known, encompassing laws of energy and frequency. Everything and everyone is made up of energy; therefore, it follows that everything has a frequency. This includes each and every part of our bodies, down to the molecular level, including every one of our thoughts.

The laws regarding magnets, attraction, energy, and frequency are generally accepted. When it comes to believing these laws also apply to our individual lives, however, many resist these truths. But no matter what we choose to believe, these laws do exist and they affect every aspect of our lives. They influence what we draw to ourselves, manipulate our moods, manifest and create all that surrounds us.

Accepting these laws as truths is especially difficult when we find ourselves in challenging or difficult states. When we worry and obsess over our situation we drown any hope or possible solution in a sea of depression. One-way to work toward the surface, to a positive state of mind, is to write and/or repeat, "Thank you for the positive outcome to…." or "I am grateful and happy because…" These statements place your problems in the past because when we recite these statements, we are sending out positive thoughts and attracting positive energy. Soon these good thoughts become good feelings that manifest into good things. Remember to concentrate only on the final result, and not on how it will come about. The way will become evident or appear from a source you may never expect; either way, the end result should be your only focus.

We all know people who seem to live charmed lives. Whatever they want seems to appear, many times effortlessly, as if by magic. The magic is in their minds. They think about what they want, they believe they deserve it; then they feel and visualize already having it. They are absolutely confident that it is theirs to have and in no time at all, they do! Our minds are the true source of creativity — they create everything in our world!

> "Whatever the mind can conceive and believe, it can achieve."
> ~ *Napoleon Hill, American self-help author, 1883-1970*

WARM WONDERFUL WATER

For most, relaxing in a warm bath is soothing. Many bath products, including foaming baths, body washes, and the like are available in an array of calming fragrances. If you use a bubble bath look at and play with the bubbles; it's fun and can transport you to memories of blowing bubbles as/or with a child. You may also decide to burn a scented candle. Close your eyes as you listen to peaceful music and feel the silkiness and warmth of the water. Allow your attention to be drawn to every aspect of this experience created by and for you.

Water is the most receptive of all elements and our bodies are approximately 60 percent water. This means our bodies are very receptive, too. Imagine how wonderful you would feel if you treated your body with the same consideration and thought that you put into preparing your perfect bath. Your body is a wonderful and receptive vessel. Enjoy the majesty of every fiber of your being.

> "Water is the driving force of all nature."
> **~ Leonardo da Vinci**

A BOX OF PASTRIES

If you're not convinced that our thoughts create feelings and feelings produce actions or things, think about this:

My daughter was having a few friends over and wanted to serve pastries. Funds were low so she bought a box of day-old pastries from a local grocer. It was a thin pink cardboard box with a cellophane insert in the top so you could view the contents.

She made the choice to present these treats in the best light possible. She lovingly placed each pastry on an individual dessert plate, sprinkled them with a touch of powdered sugar and drizzled chocolate sauce over that. They looked divine. Everyone was very impressed with the care my daughter put into the special desserts and couldn't stop talking about how wonderful they looked and tasted!

She could have simply placed the open box on the table or piled the pastries together on a large plate. However, the care and attention given to each pastry made it special thereby letting her guests know they were special to her, too.

Which presentation would you prefer: an open box of pastries, pastries piled together on a single plate, or individual pastries presented with care? How would each presentation affect your feelings toward your host and in turn develop into how you think your host feels about you?

Given these examples it's easy to understand that our thoughts create our feelings. We can transform the ordinary into the extraordinary with a small bit of attention. It doesn't matter if you view a situation from a caring, positive point of view or from an uncaring or negative point of view; whatever you think, good, bad or indifferent, your thoughts create your feelings and manifest into reality.

Since we view everything in our world as a positive or negative, this must include the people in our lives as well as ourselves. How we perceive ourselves leads to how we present our lives and ourselves. For instance, our resumes place us in the most positive light possible. If we choose to present our challenges as strength building and simply different ways of doing things, others will, too. To be viewed as a strong or courageous person is far better than being pitied for having to adjust to a different or more challenging way of living. Find and/or create the positives in your life! Present yourself well and inspire hope.

> "Focus on the positives and be grateful."
> ~ *Katrina Bowden*

WHEN THE WORLD WAS BLACK AND WHITE!

It's true that perceptions of the same event can differ completely from person to person, so how do we know what truly is — or does that even matter? I believe the only reality that matters is the one we believe to be true. Because how we perceive our individual realities influences how we relate to the rest of the world, for better or worse.

What follows is an actual and surprising conversation with my five-year-old grandson. He wanted to know how old my father, his great-grandfather, was going to be on his upcoming birthday.

He asked, "How old is Pa going to be?"

"Pa will be seventy-five," I replied with a smile.

He looked surprised and said, "Oh, that means Pa was alive when the world was black and white."

It took a moment before I realized the only reference my grandson had to that time period was his favorite black-and-white movie *Abbott and Costello Meet Frankenstein.* Since today's films are in color and the movies of the past are black and white, he logically thought the world must have been black and white, too.

What an amazing lesson on how our experience and knowledge dictates our views. Now, how can this lesson serve us? Simply put, we need to look at everything with new eyes, thinking outside the norm. Consider new or varied uses for ordinary items or ways to accomplish things differently. This will clear the way for fresh ideas on how to relish life and fulfill our needs. Enjoy your new eyes.

> "Perspective is everything when you are experiencing the challenges of life."
> ~ *Joni Eareckson Tada*

WHAT MAKES THEM HAPPY?

Some folks are happy living a meager existence with none of the trappings of a modern lifestyle. They smile and enjoy every aspect of their lives. If it rains, they're grateful for the water and if it's warm and sunny, it's a perfect time to hang clothes out to dry or plan an outdoor event. In everything they find pleasure, a blessing to be grateful for. They view their lives, the people in them, and all that surrounds them with gratitude. Simply living is joyful.

For others, modern trappings become traps propelling them to want more. Before they know it, their time is spent working to pay or care for their possessions. Things become more important than enjoying our magical world and all it has to offer. Unfortunately, it's also true that there are times the important people in their lives take a back seat to their possessions. Keeping up with the Joneses isn't all it's cracked up to be.

When my brain tumors were discovered and the reality that my life was in danger, my loved ones entered my mind. I thought about the opportunities I missed to share time with them. My possessions never entered my mind! What will you think about?

> "Wealth is the ability to fully experience life."
> *~ Henry David Thoreau*

LESSONS FROM THE BIG SCREEN

Movies often hold unexpected lessons. Here are two movie clips I fell in love with because of the great meanings they convey.

The first is, sadly, a deleted scene. The power and lesson it holds touched my very core. It's from the movie *Bruce Almighty*, which was released as a drama/fantasy in 2003. It starred Jim Carrey as Bruce Nolan, a fed-up news reporter who was passed over for an anchorman position on the news. Jennifer Aniston played Grace Connelly, Bruce's loving girlfriend who always looked for the good in others and truly believed in God. She tried to help Bruce but her efforts often failed because he viewed his life in such a negative way. Morgan Freeman played God, who went to Bruce after Bruce complained that God was treating him poorly. God planned to give Bruce all his powers since Bruce believed he could do God's job better. Bruce's new powers only extended through his city but as it turned out, even that was an enormous and overwhelming job.

Bruce decided to simplify things by answering "Yes" to everyone's prayers. This turned his city into utter chaos. Once again Bruce called on God, this time to fix the mess he'd created with all the "Yes" answers. The scene went as follows:

Bruce gave Filbert Davis, a chunky kid who was constantly teased because of his inability to climb a rope in gym class, the strength to climb the rope, thereby changing the course of his life by this one event.

God said, "You remember Filbert Davis; he was a brilliant young man who was going to be a great poet. The soul of his work would have been built around his childhood pain. Now he's headed for a career as a professional wrestler. He will eventually test positive for steroids and end up managing a muffler shop."

Bruce responded, "Well, that's a disappointment."

God said, "He got what he prayed for. You see, Bruce, triumph is born out of struggle, faith is the alchemist. If you want to paint pictures like this, you have to use some dark colors."

Morgan Freeman's lines as God are so true and powerful. We never know how the dark times in our lives will benefit others or us in the future. Gaining the knowledge that we survived difficult times is a testament to our strength. Proof that we can succeed no matter what!

The second movie is *Return to Me*. It was a 2000 melodrama/drama starring David Duchovny as Bob Rueland. He was a contractor whose wife died and her organs were donated to others. Minnie Driver starred as Grace Briggs, a talented young painter who desperately needed a new heart. Carroll O'Connor starred as Grace's grandfather, Marty O'Reilly.

To set the scene: Grace and Bob met and fall in love. Grace then discovers that the heart she received was from Bob's wife. She was brokenhearted and couldn't believe the cruel trick life had played on her. She knew she couldn't keep this information from Bob. Grace discussed her dilemma with her grandfather.

He told her, "It's the character that's the strongest, that God gives the most challenges to. Now you can take that as a compliment."

To see our lives through this description will benefit anyone going through life's difficult challenges. I never thought of my character as being overly strong or my challenges as a form of a compliment, but it definitely helps to do so.

THE THREE THINGS

Life has granted me many lessons and without the following three things I have no doubt that my life would have been and would continue to be much more difficult. The three things you need not only to survive but also thrive are Knowledge, Faith, and a Sense of Humor.

1. **KNOWLEDGE**

    Knowledge brings understanding. Everyone wants to be understood and to understand what he or she is going through. Understanding leads to compassion; compassion for others but just as important, for ourselves. Sadly, the sayings, "I'm my harshest critic," and "I'm my own worst enemy," are often true. Most of us give more time, devotion, and compassion to those we love and to absolute strangers than we afford ourselves. We are the only ones with the power to change this.

....

"The good life is one inspired by love and guided by knowledge."
~ *Bertrand Russell*

....

2. FAITH

When I speak of Faith I'm not referring to a specific religion but the absolute belief that what you are facing has a reason. A reason you may never understand or even know, but a reason nonetheless. That Faith will you make it through tough times.

....

"You Either Have Faith or Fear, not Both."
From Marlo Morgan's book, The Mutant Message Down Under

....

3. A SENSE OF HUMOR

Have a Sense of Humor about your situation and yourself. We laugh at 'slapstick comedy,' when someone is hit in the face with a pie or trips and falls. Unfortunately, we rarely laugh at our own situations and ourselves. If we trip and fall we gauge our embarrassment by the number of people who witnessed it. When I trip or fall I prefer to laugh. It's great to see the reaction of those witnessing my fall. Instead of turning away to hide their smile or muffle their laughter, we laugh together and no one is embarrassed!

Smiling and laughter brings us relief while existing in a depressed or stressful state for long periods of time is debilitating and extremely unhealthy. Fill your life with laughter.

....

"A person without a sense of humor is like a wagon without springs. It's jolted by every pebble on the road."
~ Henry Ward Beecher

....

Section Three

COMFORTING IDEAS

TEDDY BEARS

Teddy bears or other stuffed animals are great. They are an excellent outlet for anger and a comfort when you just need something to hold on to. Pick up a favorite toy just for you. Hug, hit, or throw your toy; it's all up to you and no one gets hurt. Besides, stuffed animals are very forgiving.

ANIMAL MAGIC

Animals bring joy, comfort, and are often therapeutic. Horseback riding, working with dolphins, or other helper dogs and animals is wonderfully freeing. Investigate available animal programs, as the benefits are worthwhile. Pets give us unconditional love and provide us with a friend to love and care for. If you don't own a pet, visiting zoos or animal sanctuaries is a delightful way to enjoy a little animal magic. Watching wildlife shows or reading books about your favorite animal is also enjoyable.

WARM BLANKETS

Remember to surround yourself with the coziness and warmth of a favorite throw, blanket, or bath towel. There's nothing like snuggling up in a velvety soft fabric to relax and soothe our bodies and minds. We all deserve a cozy luxury in our lives.

HUGS AND SMILES

Giving and receiving a hug that lasts at least twenty seconds brings feelings of contentment, security, and sincere well-being. Give a heartfelt hug; the mutual feelings it creates will amaze you.

The same is true of a genuine smile. The simple act of smiling positively affects your entire body. Smile at a complete stranger; it may be just what they need and it will do you good, too.

FULL SPECTRUM LIGHTING

People who live in cloudy rainy areas often suffer with depression. Trips to tanning beds are often recommended and referred to as Sunshine Therapy. This type of treatment is beneficial for many. If you reside in a sunny place, going outside to soak up the sunshine and vitamin D is a natural way to improve your outlook.

FAVORITE SCENTS

Aromatherapy is helpful for many. The smell of lavender is used to relax; some even apply a touch to their upper lip to ease or eliminate snoring. Peppermint, on the other hand, will pep us up and clear the air! In addition, the aroma of carnations is said to be very healing and is often used in 'get well' bouquets.

Smells evoke memories. Think of these aromas: fresh baked breads, cookies, pies, baked ham, roasted turkey, or a barbeque. They can bring forth thoughts of a cherished occasion or person. The scent of a particular perfume or aftershave may also remind you of a particular person. Take the time to breathe in the fragrances of life.

TOUCH AND TASTE

The luxurious feel of silk or other fine fabrics can be comforting, exciting, or even sensual. But it doesn't stop there. What about the feel of wood, the petals of a flower, the silkiness of soap, the softness of a marshmallow, the warmth of a fire, the refreshment of a cool breeze, the hand of someone you love? The pleasure to touch is all around us.

Savoring the taste of a preferred dish delights the taste buds, reminds us of days gone by and creates new memories. In past times, having dinner was an event. Families and friends gathered and mealtimes were opportunities to share and care for one another. Nowadays, the fifteen-minute fast food dinner seems to be the norm for many. In fact, many barely taste their food, much less enjoy it. Slow down, sit down at a table, and treat yourself to the enticing flavors of life.

Simple pleasures of touch and taste can make every day a celebration.

MUSIC

Waking to your favorite music is a wonderful way to begin the day and so much nicer than waking up to the blaring buzz of an alarm clock. Being jolted from sleep by an alarm is the job of a smoke detector warning us of danger and certainly not a comforting way to wake on a daily basis. I've personally never understood how an annoyingly loud noise could be good for anyone, much less a soothing way to begin one's day. ALARM clock says it all!

Listening to lovely music throughout the day is quite enjoyable as we often relate specific times and people to certain songs. Hearing a special tune can draw us back to a tender memory of a blissful period of life. Singing or humming along is nice, too.

Besides listening to music, play an instrument you know or learn to play a new one. No matter what you choose, developing a musical skill takes time and can be an exciting challenge and most rewarding.

FUN IN EVERY ROOM

I have something in every room of our home that brings a smile. The item doesn't have to be large, just something that reminds you of a happy memory or is a bit silly. These things will always lift your spirit; even if you don't consciously recognize the cheerful item it will affect your subconscious favorably.

GREEN THUMB, HAPPY HEART

It's wonderfully satisfying to care for and watch plants mature. This can be done on any scale, indoor or out. Indoor spaces can host a variety of plants, including Bonsai trees, assorted flowers, cacti, succulents, herbs, fruits, and vegetables. Small outdoor spaces can be used for raised bed gardens or hanging baskets while larger exterior spaces are great for trees, bushes, and larger plant varieties. Visit a local nursery to decide which plants appeal to you. Always keep in mind a plant's needs, from the type of soil, fertilizer, light, drainage, space, and mature size.

The feel of rich earth is very grounding—pun intended. And this pleasure often ignites memories of playing in mud puddles or sand boxes. There's also the joy of picking foods and eating them before they reach the kitchen. Whatever your space, the joy of a single potted plant or vase of flowers can excite the senses.

PEACEFUL NATURE

Walking, hiking, biking, swimming, or simply sitting outdoors is revitalizing. Gazing at the sky's ever-changing canvas of moving colors at sunrise or sunset is pure magic. If it's windy, close your eyes and listen. Is that the sound of the wind as it weaves its way through the trees or is it a stream or waterfall nearby? With our eyes closed we can imagine whichever we prefer. Deeply breathe in the fresh air and scents nature has to offer.

If the weather isn't favorable, watch or read about a place you love. Today, recordings are available of the sounds of rain falling, a crackling fire, ocean waves lapping the shore, birds chirping, rainforest and even dolphin or whale sounds. There are also DVDs available with continuous running fireplaces and fish tanks; both instantly change the mood of the room. Many of us happily live in the boxes we've created for ourselves, yet instinctively we all hear the call of nature and want to connect with the earth in some way. Treat yourself to nature's wonder.

ARTS AND CRAFTS

Visiting art galleries, working as an artist or on a craft project can fill many hours with pleasure and may be a source of income. Simply coloring in a coloring book or doodling on a blank sheet can release your creative side and take your mind off your worries. If you're not sure what might interest you, visit a hobby shop or try a few classes. Besides, it's also a wonderful way to meet new friends.

STORY GAME

Playing the story game with a group of friends is a nice way to spend time together. Everyone sits in a circle or around a table to watch each other's reactions. Choose a person, place, event, or genre. This can be accomplished by having separate containers filled with scraps of paper, each listing several different types of people, places, events, and genres. Have someone choose a scrap of paper from each container to create your scene. Decide on a length of time or the number of times to go around the circle. Next ask each person to add a sentence or two to the story. The fun comes from never knowing how a story will unfold or end. Every story will be different and it's a great way to stretch your imagination.

MANI/PEDI

Whether male or female, tending to your hands, feet, and nails is a necessary part of having a healthy body. No matter if you care for yourself or go to a salon, soaking your hands and feet is very calming. Topping off a manicure with a clear coat of polish gives a sleek well-groomed look to men and women's hands alike.

If you choose to paint your nails, have fun picking a color or design. Go wild; what do you have to lose? It's only polish and it can provide a constant source of delight. As teenagers, my sister and I would have fun painting each nail a different color, or we might add polka dots or lines to individual nails. It was a nice way to spend time together and every time I looked at my hands it reminded me of the fun we shared and always brought a smile to my face. Laugh at the simple pleasures like multi-colored nails.

MASSAGES

Massage therapy benefits our mind, body, and spirit. Depending on your physical needs, you may desire a gentle massage or you may require a deep tissue massage. Whatever your choice or needs may be, staying well hydrated and resting after each session will bring about the best possible outcome.

RESTFUL SLEEP

"One more hour of work and then I'll go to sleep." "I only have one more load of laundry and the dishes to clear up and then I'll hit the sack." Sound familiar? Sadly, rest is something that falls to the bottom of the list of important things to do. This lack of sleep will eventually catch up with all of us. We are not robots and mistakes are made when we are over-tired. Each of us has an internal clock, and our needed hours of rest may vary; respect that and care for you first. Make your bedroom an inviting place of comfort and snuggle in for a good long rest. The world will be there when you wake up and will look much brighter after a good night's sleep.

HEALTH AND EXERCISE

Our health is negatively affected by stress. Living in a stressful state for long periods of time causes uneasy feelings; dis-ease causes disease. And incurable can mean curable from within. This is proven by the 'Placebo Effect.' A patient is given a basic sugar pill (placebo) and is told it's a cure; low and behold, the patient recovers aided only by a sugar pill and the amazing power of the mind.

Consult your physician and start an exercise program. Exercising not only helps us physically but also releases endorphins, making us feel good emotionally. Besides, as Katherine Hepburn once said, "If you rest, you rust."

CONSUME HEALTHY FOOD

If under a doctor's care, follow the diet prescribed. If you're not, pay attention to your body's needs. For most it's a good idea to eat only healthy and non-processed foods avoiding sugar, preservatives, and chemicals. It's also wise to eat only complex carbohydrates and to consume them in moderation.

I personally prefer organic foods, and free range, antibiotic free meats whenever possible. Consuming processed sugar negatively affects my eyesight and hormonal hot flashes.

Fitness guru Jack LaLanne was reported to have said, "If it's made by man or in a can, don't eat it." Now this may be taking things a bit far but eating as naturally as we can is beneficial to our bodies as well as our state of mind.

AVOID ALCOHOL AND DEPRESSANTS

Alcohol and other depressants should be avoided at all costs. This advice should be obvious, but sometimes we're put in social situations or feel a bit down and think an alcoholic drink will help; actually, it has the opposite effect. Instead, keep a variety of your favorite non-alcoholic beverages handy. You may also want to implement some of the suggestions in this book. For example, recite the positives in your life or do something else that lifts your spirit.

'NO' IS NOT A DIRTY WORD

It's wonderful to help others but it's just as important to know when our energy reserves are down and 'no' is the appropriate response for our health and well-being. The important part of saying no is to feel comfortable with your decision. Guilt has no place in this. You're taking care of yourself so you can be of service later. Do what you're able and be good to yourself.

EMOTIONAL VAMPIRES

Emotional vampires are people who literally suck the energy from our bodies. They drone on and on about their horrible situations, dismissing anything positive we may have to offer. Trying to keep them up will drain our positive reserves to nothing. Give your friend or loved one the energy you can spare, listen, sympathize, offer hope, and wish them well but protect yourself. Just as we are instructed on an airplane, "Put on your oxygen mask first, then assist others." You will be of no value if you're too weak to even help yourself.

We all need to vent once in awhile and it's healthy to do so. It's not healthy for you or anyone else to live in a negative state of mind for long periods of time. Be kind to yourself and surround yourself with upbeat people.

LIMIT NEGATIVE NEWS

Avoid listening to a lot of news; being informed doesn't have to mean being inundated with negativity. Most news reports events of the past or warns us of things most individuals do not have the power to change. This lack of power or control may create or add to fear and depression.

WORDS OF WISDOM

Adding positive quotes, affirmations, or prayers throughout your home is a wonderful way to remind yourself of the good in life. Many quotes have been passed down through the ages and the truths they hold will forever ring true. Place a favorite where you'll see it when you wake. It's a marvelous way to begin each day. You may want to carry a few favorites with you. Referring to them will help in troubled times.

IN THIS MOMENT IN TIME

In this moment in time, you are all right, you are reading or listening to this book, and it's impossible to know what the next hour or day will hold. Still right here in this moment you are OK so enjoy it. My vision is uncertain and I don't know when or if it will completely be gone. Being miserable because of this uncertainty would be a gigantic waste of time. Instead, I joyfully appreciate every minute of sight. Life offers no guarantees and once a moment has passed it's gone forever. Make the best of what you currently have and relish your time.

CELEBRATE EVERY DAY

Using things that are dear to you daily or wearing a favorite piece of jewelry or item of clothing can do wonders for your spirit. You may want to carry a special object with you, perhaps a lucky charm, a small remembrance or photo of a certain person, place, or event. It simply needs to be something that brings a smile. Even a simple strand of Mardi gras beads hanging where you'll see them is a great reminder to celebrate every day.

> "Time cannot be replaced. Spend it wisely by filling every possible moment with special people and things that bring you pleasure!"
> ~ Cynthia L. De Boer

LIVE IN HOPE

Living in hope will reveal possibilities. We can't choose much of what life throws at us but we can decide how to react. When times are tough it's hard to sit back and view our troubles without emotional turmoil, but it's vitally important to do so. We need to examine our thoughts and feelings to judge whether they are serving us in a positive or healthy manner. If not, we must change them by exploring any good that may arise from our situation. The experience may open doors to new ways of doing certain things or force us to utilize items we never thought of.

We journey this earth together and it's possible that meeting a new person is part of the reason for our dilemma. Not everything that happens to us benefits us. Perhaps our situation is meant to help someone else, either by offering them the chance to assist us or by letting them know there's someone else who understands what they are experiencing. After all, we may be the exact person someone else needs. Offering hope or ideas to another benefits them but is just as rewarding to us. Sharing thoughts and feelings builds understanding and hope, thereby allowing possibilities to emerge. Our thoughts become feelings and feelings create all that surrounds us; in essence, our very reality. Remember, your mind holds the key to unlocking the positives in life. Make the most of it.

> "Optimism is the faith that leads to achievement. Nothing can be done without hope and confidence."
> ~ *Helen Keller*

Section Four

YOUR GROUNDWORK

This section contains helpful exercises. In many, I instruct you to record or write down your thoughts. Although I have provided blank pages to do so, you may want to keep a notebook and pen or tape recorder nearby. Recording thoughts the moment they arise enables us to remember them. Please feel free to customize each exercise to fit your particular needs.

> "Your mind will answer most questions if you learn to relax and wait for the answer."
> **~ William S. Burroughs**

JOURNALING

Journaling is an excellent outlet for relieving stress. It helps us analyze our thoughts and often brings our fears into their proper perspective. Once they're written on the page they become a wonderful source of reflection. You will discover many of your past concerns never came to be or if they did, they often turned out far better than expected. Past entries log difficult times and are the absolute proof that you met and survived those challenges. This gives you the courage needed to believe you can meet and succeed no matter what you currently face.

Journaling is very beneficial, and of course, is for your eyes only. You can write whatever you feel without fear of being judged.

> "I'm always trying to figure out ways to keep hold of memories. My one-sentence journal, for instance."
> ~ *Gretchen Rubin*

Take a moment and write a few thoughts that are currently running through your mind:

STORY WRITING

Writing stories using your troubles as your character's problems is another wonderful stress reliever. Writing in this manner will enable you to look at your challenges from outside yourself. In a sense, you are giving your problems away. As a writer, you will want to offer hope to your character, which opens your mind to explore numerous outcomes and possible options you might not have otherwise discovered. It's a chance to 'Live in Hope!' You might also develop a bit more compassion for yourself through your characters for yourself.

Sharing your story with others to gain their insights to your characters' plight while retaining your anonymity is another option.

*****

"Writers are like Gods on paper because they create worlds with their pens."
~ Cynthia L. De Boer

To get a feel for this type of writing, add a few sentences to the following lines: "(She or He) faced many problems in the past and tenaciously conquered them all. Now (he or she) is facing her next challenge …"

ACCOMPLISHMENT LIST

Make a list of your accomplishments from the smallest achievements to the major successes in your life. This serves as excellent proof of your strength and the amazing feats you've already achieved. It helps to open your mind to hope and future possibilities.

> "As for accomplishments,
> I just did what I had to do
> as things came along."
> ~ *Eleanor Roosevelt*

Begin your list by writing down five accomplishments.

1.

2.

3.

4.

5.

RECITING AND WRITING GRATITUDE LISTS

Close your eyes and take deep breaths while reciting your pleasures and/or blessings. Consciously feel the feelings of gratitude and joy for each one. Holding a simple stone or other item may increase your ability to concentrate on each item as you recite your list. In fact, you may want to carry that item with you as a constant reminder.

You may prefer to write down and read your 'Gratitude List.' A list is a physical reminder and can be carried with you. Refer to it as often as you like and add to your list as more blessings come to mind.

The best way to begin your list is to write whatever comes to mind. Do not concern yourself with placing them in any particular order as you can rewrite it in any order you choose. Patterns emerge as you discover many blessings are because of someone in your life or come from a particular part of your life. It's enlightening to see where your joy comes from and gives you a great sense of appreciation for those people and areas of your life. The feelings of true gratitude are so positive that it's impossible to be depressed when you sincerely feel thankful for all you have.

> "Gratitude is the fairest blossom which springs from the soul."
> ~ *Henry Ward Beecher*

Quickly record ten things for which you are grateful and then continue until you've reached one hundred (on a separate piece of paper). Don't be concerned with repeats or placing them in a specific order — just write and you'll discover definite patterns.

1.   2.

3.   4.

5.   6.

7.   8.

9.   10.

DEVELOP A HEALTHY RESPECT FOR YOURSELF

If you find it difficult to believe you are extraordinary, think of the special people in your life. I'm sure you hold them in high regard so why is it so hard to believe they feel the same way about you? Look at yourself as if you were observing a friend. Reflect on all you've accomplished, the people you've touched, and your abilities. I'm sure you will discover you're quite an amazing human being, someone worthy of your genuine and healthy respect.

> "Respect for self is the beginning of cultivating virtue in men and women."
> *~ Gordon B. Hinckley*

Write down five of your attributes and why they are worthy of praise. You may want to add how they have benefited or influenced your actions or the actions of someone else. If you need inspiration refer to your list of accomplishments or your resume. Increase the number of reasons/attributes you possess as they come to mind. Before you know it, you'll impress yourself!

1.

2.

3.

4.

5.

HEART TO HEART TALKS

Having a heart-to-heart conversation with yourself can be quite beneficial. Pretend you're talking to a friend who is in your situation. What positive advice and guidance would you offer to help him or her feel better? Remember your words and repeat them aloud several times back to yourself. It will do wonders.

> "My best friend is the one who brings out the best in me."
> *~ Henry Ford*

Picture your best friend in your mind and imagine he or she has your troubles. Without hesitation, begin speaking, "I love you and it hurts to see you in so much distress. You are going to make it through this because…"

WHOM WOULD YOU INVITE?

Imagine you are to be presented with an award and are able to invite ten people to the event. Whom would you choose? We all have people in our lives but many may not view us with the same level of importance as we place on them. Think of the people who would feel honored to attend and celebrate you.

When your list is complete, these are the people you should remain close to. It truly doesn't matter how or if they are related. It does matter that they care about you, would support you, and share your joy. The wonderful people willing to make you a priority are to be treasured and honored. They are true blessings. Keep them close.

> "The people in your life are important. Meaningful relationships with those people are very important."
> *~ Ed Bradley*

Make your list and keep these people close.

1.

2.

3.

4.

5.

6.

7.

8

9.

10.

SUPPORT GROUPS

Support groups are an outstanding source for information and emotional support. People sharing the same experiences often have an easier time relating to one another and revealing their true feelings. These discussions often open the door to enabling them to share thoughts and feelings with family and friends outside the situation. Visit a few groups to discover which ones appeals to you and fit your specific needs.

"Support systems and support groups are so important because that's what makes you stronger."
~ *Nikki Bella*

If you know of a few support groups, record them below, then add names of friends, family, and associates who may offer other ideas to you. There is space below for five options.

1.

2.

3.

4.

5.

LAUGHTER

Watching children's movies and/or comedies, reading or telling jokes are simply fun! Visiting a local improv show is also delightful. Research has shown that a smile or positive feeling is much more powerful than a frown or negative feeling. Being joyful for an additional five or ten minutes per day will have an amazing transformative effect. Smile and laugh as often as possible.

"Laughter is an instant vacation."
~ *Milton Berle*

Think back to enjoyable times and make a list of five. It's always great to revisit fun places and events.

1.

2.

3.

4.

5.

DOING FOR OTHERS

Think of something nice to do for someone else and put all your energy into that. Assisting others is very rewarding and takes your mind off your own troubles. It's a surefire way to brighten your mood while lifting someone else's spirit. Volunteer your time, visit a homeless shelter or donate something to a favorite charity, group or church. When you give someone a gift, they are happy to be remembered and their gratitude fills you with the pleasure and the satisfaction that comes from giving.

> "What a man does for others,
> not what they do for him,
> gives him immortality."
> *~ Daniel Webster*

Take a few minutes and think of others in need of a pick-me-up. Perhaps they need a hand to hold, a shoulder to lean on or assistance with a project. You may be able to arrange a special outing or make an upcoming birthday or special day even more cheerful and memorable. Record ideas below:

1.

2.

3.

4

5.

BREATHE DEEPLY

Breathing deeply can calm nerves and relax you. The first technique is to breathe in through your nose to the count of four and then release the breath through your mouth to the count of four. Repeat ten times and do this throughout your day. Even three deep breaths will help when confronted with a stressful situation. In addition, taking a few deep breaths allows time to think before acting or speaking. This delay will help prevent explosions of actions or words that are impossible to retrieve, as we can't rewind time.

The second technique I wish to share will assist you in relaxing into a peaceful sleep. Begin at your toes; tense them and then release the tension. Work your way up your body, tensing and then releasing the tension from your feet, ankles, and calves, continuing up your body. Once you've arrived at your neck, take a deep breath and evaluate if there are any areas of your body that still contain stress; if so, repeat the exercise. Once you're as relaxed as possible, place your hands on your stomach and concentrate on your breathing. Count each breath — breath one, breath two, breath three — and repeat the process until you doze off. Of course, adjustments can made to fit your particular disability. Think of ways to use the above techniques and breathe your way to peace.

> "An inspiration — a long, deep breath of the pure air of thought — could alone give health to the heart."
> *~ Richard Jefferies*

Stop and take a few moments to practice the first breathing exercise and continue to do so throughout the day. Keep this book handy when you head off to bed; practice the second technique.

MEDITATION OR PRAYER

Positive meditation and/or prayer are extremely valuable. Generally, when we pray it's for our personal benefit or for someone close to us. We want to eliminate any hardships but we need to remember negatives often result in learning or gaining something positive. When praying or meditating in request for anyone or anything, I begin by reciting, "For the best and highest for all concerned." Remember, we journey together.

It's also true that when we request answers, yes is preferable. We can also handle an occasional no; however, the answer that is the hardest to accept is 'wait.' We want definite answers, not a wait-and-see. While waiting can be difficult, we can be comforted in the knowledge that events unfold as they should and in the time that's required. Static periods offer a time to recharge, think, and for other events to transpire, making the wait completely worthwhile. Reviewing our past will often reveal projects that were delayed actually came out better than anticipated because of the extended time to completion.

> "Meditation is the soul's perspective glass."
> ~ *Owen Feltham*

Close your eyes and begin by thinking of something positive in your life and meditate or give thanks in the form of a prayer. This only takes a few moments and is a great way to become comfortable with the process. As you gain comfort and confidence, extend your meditation time. Incorporate at least fifteen minutes a day to this practice and you will enrich your life with peace.

'DON'T WANTS' REVEAL 'TRUE WANTS'

Many times, it's easier to know what we don't want than to acknowledge what we do. For example: When asked what we would prefer for dinner, we say anything will do. But if we're asked if liver and onions is okay and it's a dish we don't care for, it's very easy to say no.

One way to decide what we want is to divide a paper in half and write Don't Want on one side and Do Want on the other. As you list the things you do not want, your true desires will become evident. Once your lists are complete, tear the sheet in half and destroy the Don't Want side. Save, read, feel, believe, and visualize your true wants. Soon they will materialize.

Remember to only focus on the positive. No matter what you think and feel, whether it's negative or positive — it will be drawn to you. You are the magnet!!

"All that we are is the result of what we have thought. The mind is everything. What we think we become."
~ *Buddha*

Record the things you DO NOT want on one side of the paper; this will help you uncover what you do want.

I DO **NOT** WANT...   I **DO** WANT...

1.   1.

2.   2.

3.   3.

4.   4.

5.   5.

TRACK AND TRANSFORM NEGATIVES INTO POSITIVES

When saying or thinking a negative thought concerning something you're afraid may happen in the future or something you wish to change, reverse the negative by adding a positive statement. If it's a worry about a current situation or a concern from the past, add the phrase "… in the past." to the thought or statement, thereby placing it firmly behind you. For example, change "I am depressed" to "In the past I was depressed." It's obvious that by merely saying something doesn't automatically make it so, but if you say it often enough you will begin to believe it, feel it, and it will become true.

Words become thoughts and thoughts become feelings. Several times a day schedule a few moments to reflect on the past hour or two. Think about your feelings, the way you reacted, the words you used, and if you experienced moments of joy. You may want to record your thoughts in a journal or on tape. Charting your days will give you an accurate view of how you truly feel. You will be able to see what brings you happiness and how you may alter your words, reactions, and thereby your feelings to create a happier life.

> "Words, so powerful, they can crush a heart or heal it. They can shatter dreams or energize them. They can obstruct connection or invite it. They can create defenses or melt them. We have to use words wisely."
> ~ *J. Brown*

Concentrate on your words, thoughts, and feelings throughout the day. Every time you say or think something negative immediately follow the thought with a positive statement. Record or write only the positive statements in the space below or in a notebook. This will help you train your mind to stay in a more positive place.

1.

2.

3.

4.

5.

SET A SCHEDULE

Time is an irreplaceable commodity. By creating a schedule, we give our time importance, a purpose, or reason to spend it wisely instead of letting it waste away. Schedules motivate us and keep us on track. They keep us looking forward into the future instead of fretting about the past. Remember to include 'Do Nothing Days' in your schedule. Days to relax and recharge are important to every aspect of our being.

"Time cannot be replaced. Spend it wisely by filling every possible moment with special people and things that bring you pleasure!"
~ *Cynthia L. De Boer*

If you do not have a calendar, use the space below to jot down your daily activities. Examples: time for personal care, meal times, times for shopping and other errands, time to spend with friends; time set aside for hobbies and favorite TV shows or media events.

After completing your list, think and add other activities to enrich your days. The same old, same old can become quite dreary and can lead to sadness or a state of depression.

RELISH THE UNEXPECTED

There are times when our plans don't exactly work out as we expect. A missed turn or forgotten stop can take us to the unexpected. You never know what you may encounter. Instead of being irritated, look for the possibilities.

For me, a missed turn meant I went to my fourth scheduled stop before my third stop. This change in plans steered me to a visit with a friend I hadn't seen in over a year. It was a delightful surprise and one that wouldn't have occurred without the missed turn.

"To expect the unexpected shows a thoroughly modern intellect."
~ *Oscar Wilde*

As you think back to unexpected events in your life, record them below. This exercise will allow you to see the wonder in missed turns and delayed schedules.

1.

2.

3.

4.

5.

FIND YOUR BLISS

We all need to feel useful, to have a goal or purpose. Give yourself something to look forward to. Here are some potential options: Preparing for an upcoming visit or outing is often half the fun. Working on a hobby, playing a game, or going out for a bit of 'consumer therapy' is always nice. It's fun to indulge ourselves or someone else to a special something. Spend time with the important people in your life. Creating a memory book by adding captions to photos or recording your thoughts on a video or tape machine allows you to relive times we may have forgotten. Exploring the pleasures of our past can reveal hobbies or the simpler things we loved doing, many of which may still be enjoyed today. Search for the things that bring you happiness and follow your Bliss.

....

> "You change your life by
> changing your heart."
> *~ Max Lucado*

....

Use the space below to record blissful thoughts and ideas that bring a smile.

1.

2.

3.

4.

5.

ENJOY AN ACTIVITY

I love to swing; for me it's such a happy and exhilarating feeling. This comes from my youth and although I may feel a little foolish swinging on a child's playground, it's a wonderful way to feel young at heart. Besides, giving someone else a reason to smile at our silliness is a great thing. It's glorious to enjoy the simple pleasure of moving to and fro, reaching for the sky as the wind rushes by and then returning to earth for a repeat performance, again and again. I just love it!

> "Focus on the journey, not the destination. Joy is not found in finishing an activity but in doing it."
> *~ Greg Anderson*

**Think of simple pleasures and record them below. Have fun and don't worry about looking a bit foolish.
Laughter is contagious.**

1.

2.

3.

4.

5.

CREATE YOUR HEAVEN ON EARTH

We've all heard or seen someone whose calm nature is so peaceful we want to step inside his or her mind if only for a moment or two. We long to trade our crazy world for a peaceful beach or garden far from our daily concerns. Our amazing minds hold the key. It's been proven that whether we visually see something with our eyes or visualize it in our mind's eye our brain creates the same images, responses, and feelings throughout our bodies — it truly doesn't matter!

The following exercise will enable you to achieve peaceful slivers of time that will increase with repeated practice, no matter where you are physically.

Close your eyes and breathe deeply. Imagine a place that brings you a joyful peace. Is it daytime or nighttime, cloudy or starry? What's the weather like? Is it cool or warm, breezy or calm? Visualize every feature: its location, the colors you see, every sound you hear, the scents that fill the air, and most importantly, the feelings you feel. Hold onto every aspect of the place you've invented in your mind. Experience it as if you're physically there. Feel yourself relax with each breath, let peace surround you. Remain there observing all you've created.

While you are doing this create a key to use to open the door to your special place. You can do this by touching two fingers together you don't normally touch. For example, touch your thumb and second finger together and use this action to enter your Heaven on Earth. If this doesn't please you, decide on another discreet way to access your special place. When you're ready, open your eyes with the knowledge that your wonderful place is only a touch away. Step inside your mind whenever you need a pick-me-up, feel overwhelmed, stressed, or unhappy. It's your place — just for you. You created it and only you can change it!

"The glow of one warm thought is to me, worth more than money."
~ *Thomas Jefferson*

Design every aspect of your 'Heaven on Earth' and keep it safely locked away in your mind. Let it grow and evolve to fit your ever-changing life. Decide on a discreet key to use to access your special place. Visit your special place as often as you like.

If desired, use the space below to record some of the aspects of your special place. You may choose to draw a picture or list your desired wants. Seeing them on paper or hearing them by recording your thoughts is a helpful way to solidify your heavenly spot in your mind's eye. Have fun; it's just for you!

Section Five

INFORMATION and FAQS

Making adjustments and allowances for our disabilities is challenging for everyone involved. The amount of changes needed to create this new way of living is dependent on the severity and type of disability. Remembering back to the changes a new career entails will make this easier. Just as a work change can cause apprehension, so does adapting to a disability. Be patient with yourself and those around you. Search out and share as much knowledge as you can.

I mentioned the three things I believe we need not only to survive but also thrive in this world. The first is knowledge because it leads to understanding and compassion for yourself and others. The second is faith — not a particular religion — but the unwavering belief that what you are going through has a reason, even though you may never know what that reason is. The third is a sense of humor about yourself.

I am a legally blind, blonde, one-eyed woman. So, believe me, I've heard too many jokes to count. I'm constantly running into things on my totally blind side and because of the effects of my brain tumors I have severe headaches and at times, problems comprehending and remembering certain things. People often see me as a klutzy and very ditzy blonde, partly because my disabilities are invisible. They can't see a reason for my behavior so I must simply be a goofy woman. I've learned to laugh at myself and if the opportunity arises, I share my challenges in a lighthearted way. Sharing encourages others to reveal their personal trials and creates bonds between individual humans, each on a unique journey.

Negative beliefs and untruths often surround people with disabilities. We can correct this by learning and sharing the true facts and realities of life with a disability. Let's investigate.

GENERAL INFORMATION ON DISABILITIES

1. People with disabilities are no different from those without. They merely adapt their lives to accommodate their disability. They have hopes, dreams, families, and friends. They have intimate relationships and need the human touch just as everyone does. In short, they are normal people on this human journey.

2. Many with disabilities can manage completely on their own and prefer to do so. If you feel someone needs assistance, ask him or her before you act.

It's no different from asking people without disabilities if they need help with tasks such as carrying packages or would prefer to do it on their own.

3. The innocence of a child's questions should be encouraged. Inquiries increase knowledge for everyone around. Children and adults alike should ask questions, as this builds understanding and compassion. Besides, it's so much nicer than avoiding or placing a forbidden or taboo label on the disabled.

4. Sharing knowledge and support with others with the same disability is a wonderful way to gain insight and support. However, completely closing one's self off from the rest of the world is detrimental as it often leads to feelings of alienation. Fitting in, adjusting to, and teaching mainstream society that having a disability merely

presents a different way of living is the best for everyone.

5. People in wheelchairs are often viewed as sickly. This may come from the use of wheelchairs in hospitals and doesn't necessarily apply to the disabled. In most cases, they are just an alternate mode of transportation.

6. Again, wheelchairs are an alternate way to get around and those in them should never be viewed in a negative manner. Just as a cane, scooter, or crutches doesn't lessen a person's value, neither does a wheelchair. Common courtesy goes a long way. For instance, if an elderly person is seated it's nice to sit and engage in a conversation at his or her level rather than talking down to him or expecting her to stand. The same thing holds true for someone in a wheelchair or seated because of another challenge.

Of course, there are times we can't sit beside them, but we can make sure to maintain eye contact or even touch the person's hand or shoulder to make the connection.

7. People with limited hearing or those completely deaf can't always read lips or know sign language. These are skills and they take time to develop. If you meet someone with a hearing impairment, ask him or her how he or she prefers to communicate.

8. A white and red cane or scooter signifies that the person is legally blind. This doesn't necessarily mean they are completely without sight. The legal definition is someone with 20/200 vision or less. Simply stated, what a person with 20/20 vision can see at 200 feet has to be at 20 feet for a legally blind person to see. Sight impaired may be a better way to view this dis-

ability because of the range and types of visions issues vary widely.

9. Being legally blind doesn't necessarily mean a person is also deaf. Speaking in a louder tone may not be the best advice. When you meet a blind person, announce yourself, and ask permission to shake hands or take his or her arm. It's very unsettling to be touched or grabbed when you're not prepared.

10. People's IQ does not diminish with their sight. Just because they may take things a bit slower or appear to be unsure or their surroundings isn't proof of being mental impaired. Slowing down and feeling their way are simply ways of protecting themselves and adapting to their visual impairment.

WAYS TO PROTECT YOUR EYESIGHT

1. Regular checkups are a **MUST!**

2. If you notice any floaters, flashes of light, or dark areas, see your doctor immediately! These may be signs of a retinal issue. Retinal detachments are considered true emergencies and have to be addressed within 48 to 72 hours in order to save vision. Sadly, a detachment can lead to permanent blindness and/or the need for a prosthetic eye.

3. **Not** seeing red eyes in photos can also be a sign of a retinal issue. Visit your doctor as soon as possible.

4. Wearing dark UV sunglasses will help prevent cataracts. Before, during, and after cataract surgery, eye pressure must be monitored closely.

This will help ensure favorable and long-lasting results.

5. Any and all eye makeup should be investigated; some products for lash growth may change the color of the iris and contribute to glaucoma. Always throw out eye makeup over three months of age and/or after any type of eye infection.

6. Work accidents can often be avoided with the use of proper eye and face protection. Polycarbonate eyeglass lenses are also a good idea.

7. Wear safety goggles when using Bungee cords or any type of product that may snap back at you.

8. Many eye injuries happen from falls, so be cautious when carrying items. For example, always carry scissors with the pointed end down with your hand wrapped around the blades. Pens and pencils should also be car-

ried pointed end down as well as any other sharp object.

PROSTHETIC EYE FAQS

1. **Can you see out of your prosthetic eye?** No. A prosthetic eye is completely aesthetic. It does not function as an actual organ.

2. **How does it move?** An implant is placed in the eye socket, which the prosthetic eye is formed to fit over it, providing movement. Usually movement is a bit limited, creating the appearance of a lazy eye.

3. **Do you have to take it out at night?** Generally no, but it depends on the individual. It is recommended that prosthetic eyes be removed every six months at an ocularist's office for a polishing to remove build-up that

forms on the surface and to evaluate the fit.

4. **Are there limits to what you can do with your prosthetic eye?** Activities that put more pressure on the prosthetic eye such as skydiving, snorkeling, or riding on a rollercoaster can cause discomfort and increase mattering or discharge.

5. **Who creates prosthetic eyes?** Ocularists are the amazing, creative medical artists who fit and paint them. They go through many years of schooling and apprenticeship to develop their skills. A BCO (Board Certified Ocularist) has gone through intense training and examinations and must re-certify every six years.

6. **How long does it take to create a new eye?** A good ocularist can construct a prosthetic eye in a couple of days.

7. **How do people lose their eyes?** Medical conditions such as cancer, retinal detachments, accidents, physical abuse, and facial reconstructions are a few of the things that can cause the removal of an eye. There is no set rule for when a person should have an eye removed. Some people fight for years to keep their eyes.

8. **Why do so many people lose their eyes?** Bad things happen to good people. No one is to blame. Getting an eye removed can bring relief to people who are fighting chronic pain.

Dear Reader,

Now that you've reached the end of my book, I hope you have found it to be helpful. Whether or not you did, I would like to thank you for spending your valuable time with me. I am truly blessed to have such a fulfilling job, and I have this job because of people like you, people kind enough to give my books a chance and spend their hard-earned money buying them. For that I am eternally grateful.

If you would like to find out more about my other books, please visit my website at www.cynthialdeboer.com.

Also feel free to contact me on Facebook, Twitter, LinkedIn, YouTube or email (all details can be found on my website), as I would love to hear from you.

If you enjoyed the book and would like to help, please leave a review on Amazon, Goodreads, or anywhere else readers visit. The most important part of how well a book sells is how many positive reviews it has. By reviewing my book, you are directly helping me continue on this journey as a fulltime writer and speaker. Thanks in advance to anyone who does. It means a great deal to me!

All my best,
Cynthia L. De Boer

INDEX

Section One

MY JOURNEY AND THE NEED TO LIVE IN THE POSITIVE

Medical Challenges pg. 41

Physical Loss pg. 44

Rough Relationships pg. 45

Round Three Begins pg. 49

Trouble, Trouble Everywhere pg. 51

On to Your Journey pg. 62

Section Two

TEACHABLE MOMENTS

The Stress Cup pg. 65

Disabilities vs. Handicaps pg. 70

Excuses vs. Allowances pg. 76

We Have a Disability pg. 79

Why Am I Extremely Exhausted? pg. 86
My Father's Bed pg. 92
The Boring Body pg. 93
Healthy Respect pg. 99
A Single Crayon pg. 102
What's in the Hat? pg. 104
Wrapped in Love pg. 106
Be the Detective of Your Life! pg. 110
Purpose to Plan/ Map it Out pg. 113
Change and Magnetism pg. 116
Warm Wonderful Water pg. 119
A Box of Pastries pg. 120
When the World Was Black and White! pg. 123
What Makes Them Happy? pg. 125
Lessons from the Big Screen pg. 127
The Three Things pg. 131

Section Three

COMFORTING IDEAS

Teddy Bears pg. 135

Animal Magic pg. 135

Warm Blankets pg. 136

Hugs and Smiles pg. 137

Full Spectrum Lighting pg. 137

Favorite Scents pg. 138

Touch and Taste pg. 139

Music pg. 140

Fun in Every Room pg. 141

Green Thumb, Happy Heart pg. 141

Peaceful Nature pg. 143

Arts and Crafts pg. 144

Story Game pg. 144

Mani/Pedi pg. 145

Massages pg. 146

Restful Sleep pg. 147

Health and Exercise pg. 148

Consume Healthy Foods *pg. 149*
Avoid Alcohol and Depressants *pg. 150*
No is Not a Dirty Word *pg. 150*
Emotional Vampires *pg. 151*
Limit Negative News *pg. 152*
Words of Wisdom *pg. 152*
In This Moment in Time *pg. 153*
Celebrate Every Day *pg. 153*
Live in Hope *pg. 154*

Section Four

YOUR GROUNDWORK

Journaling pg. 158

Story Writing pg. 160

Accomplishment List pg. 162

Reciting and Writing Gratitude Lists pg. 164

Develop a Healthy Respect for Yourself pg. 167

Heart to Heart Talks pg. 169

Whom Would You Invite? pg. 171

Support Groups pg. 173

Laughter pg. 175

Doing for Others pg. 177

Breathe Deeply pg. 179

Meditation or Prayer pg. 182

Don't Wants Reveal True Wants pg. 185

Track and Transform Negatives into Positives pg. 188

Set a Schedule pg. 191

Relish the Unexpected pg. 193
Find Your Bliss pg. 195
Enjoy an Activityv pg. 197
Create Your Heaven on Earth pg. 199

Section Five

INFORMATION & FAQs

General Information of Disabilities pg. 205

Ways to Protect Your Eyesight pg. 210

Prosthetic Eye FAQs pg. 212

About the Author

Cynthia De Boer's career as an author, inspirational speaker, and disability advocate is fueled by her medical challenges, relationships, and work experiences.

Her lifelong passion for writing is echoed through Anne Frank's quote, "I can shake off everything as I write, my sorrows disappear, my courage is reborn."

Cynthia's first book *Me, Myself and Eye, The Realities of Living With a Prosthetic Eye* has been widely received as an honest and much-needed resource. Cynthia believes having a disability does not make you less of a person; it makes you more of a human being.

www.ingramcontent.com/pod-product-compliance
Lightning Source LLC
Chambersburg PA
CBHW052023070526
44584CB00016B/1875